THE CREDO SERIES

VOLUMES ALREADY PUBLISHED

THE TORCH OF LIFE:
   Continuity in Living Experience
   BY RENÉ DUBOS

OLD WINE, NEW BOTTLES:
   A Humanist Teacher at Work
   BY MOSES HADAS

MAN, NATURE AND GOD:
   A Quest for Life's Meaning
   BY F. S. C. NORTHROP

BEYOND THE CHAINS OF ILLUSION:
   My Encounter with Marx and Freud
   BY ERICH FROMM

THE CHALLENGE OF THE PASSING YEARS:
   My Encounter with Time
   BY R. M. MACIVER

OLD WINE,
NEW BOTTLES

A Humanist Teacher
at Work

BY

MOSES HADAS

 A TRIDENT PRESS BOOK
SIMON AND SCHUSTER
NEW YORK 1962

Prepared under the supervision of
POCKET BOOKS, INC.

CONTENTS

THE CREDO SERIES

Its Meaning and Function　　　　　vii
BY RUTH NANDA ANSHEN

I.	The Essential Enterprise	3
II.	What Are Humanities?	11
III.	Greek Paradigms	19
IV.	Professional and Amateur	30
V.	Bookish Evangelism	41
VI.	Saints and Fools	56
VII.	Humanist Revival	67
VIII.	Integration	85
IX.	No Trespassing	102
X.	American Renaissance	117

11138

THE CREDO SERIES

Its Meaning and Function

The Credo Series suggests that an epoch has come to an end, an epoch in which our best knowledge has been dimmed with boredom or darkened by destruction. We have felt for too long that this must be the very nature of life; this is the way life is, and to such a degree that life has consented to shrink from its own terrors, leading us to a deep apostasy of the heart and a crucifixion of our natural aspiration for experience and growth.

The absolute has surrendered to the relative. Our era of relativity, however, whether in science or in morals, does not allow us to assume that relativity implies an absence of ground to stand on, and therefore a relaxation of all effort toward foundations. "There is no firm ground," the dominant malaise of our time, this acceptance of non-finality, summons us to a heightened task. For the failure of formulated absolutes leaves the absolute requirement to evaluate again that uncaptured reality which contains and guides the total meaning of our existence.

The Credo Series hopes to unlock a consciousness that at first sight may seem to be remote but is proved on acquaintance to be surprisingly immediate since it shows the need to reconcile the life of action with the life of contemplation, practice with principle, thought with feeling, knowledge with being, and work, no longer a form of punishment as in the Judaeo-Christian tradition, but accepted as a way toward the growth and realization of the self in all its plenitude. For the whole meaning of self lies within the observer and its shadow is cast naturally on the object observed. The fragmentation of man from his work, the being of man into an eternal and temporal half, results in an estrangement of man from his creative source, from his fellows and from himself.

The symbol of *The Credo Series* is the Eye of Osiris. It is the inner Eye. Man sees in two ways: with his physical eyes, in an empirical sensing or *seeing* by direct observation, and also by an indirect envisaging. He possesses in addition to his two sensing eyes a single, image-making, spiritual and intellectual Eye. And it is the *in-sight* of this inner Eye that purifies and makes sacred our understanding of the nature of things; for that which was shut fast has been opened by the command of the inner Eye. And we become aware that to believe is to see.

Thus, it is suggested, there may be born a sharpened vision, which comes from seeing reality as the incarnation of associations and affinities with something beyond the visible self. For it is our hope to show the human relevance of ideas, the ways in which knowledge can help us to live in the immediate and real world by pointing to the confluence of man and his vocation, of subject and object, by reverencing the curious and mysterious metabolism between man and matter, the sacred nexus between the person and his work, and by asking whether the freedom now released through the creative energies of mankind will bring salvation or destruction, the answer to which will depend upon the aims we cherish.

The Credo Series submits that the universe itself is a vast entity where man will be lost if it does not converge in the person; for material forces or energies, or impersonal ideals, or scientifically objectified learning are meaningless without their relevance for human life and their power to disclose, even in the dark tendencies of man's nature, a law transcending man's arbitrariness.

For the personal is a far higher category than the abstract universal. Personality itself is an emotional, not an intellectual, experience, and the greatest achievement of knowledge is to combine the personal within a larger unity, just as in the higher stages of development the parts that make up the whole acquire greater and greater independence and individuality within the context of the whole. Reality itself is the harmony which gives to the component particulars of a thing the equilibrium of the whole. And while physical observations are ordered with direct reference to the experimental conditions, we have in sensate experience to do with separate observations whose correlation can only be indicated by their belonging to the wholeness of mind.

It is our endeavor to show that man has reached a turning point in consciousness, that his relationship with his creative self demands a clarification that can widen and deepen his understanding of the nature of reality. Work is made for man, not man for work. This Series hopes to demonstrate the sacramental character of work which is more easily achieved when the principal objects of our attention have taken on a symbolic form that is generally recognized and accepted: in other words, when there is an established iconography relating to the meaningful interpretation of man and his vocation. This suggests a "law" in the relationship of a person and his chosen discipline:

that it is valuable only when the spiritual, the creative, life is strong enough to insist on some expression through symbols. For no work can be based on material, technological or physical aspirations alone.

The human race is now entering upon a new phase of evolutionary progress, a phase in which, impelled by the forces of evolution itself, it must converge upon itself and convert itself into one single human organism dominated by a reconciliation of knowing and being in their inner unity and destined to make a qualitative leap into a higher form of consciousness that would transcend and complement individual consciousness as we know it, or otherwise destroy itself. For the entire universe is one vast field, potential for incarnation, and achieving incandescence here and there of reason and spirit. What to some is mystery and inscrutability, to others symbolizes and declares the very nature of the cosmic process. And in the whole world of *quality* with which category by the nature of our minds we necessarily make contact, we here and there apprehend pre-eminent value. This can be achieved only if we recognize that we are unable to focus our attention on the particulars of a whole without diminishing our comprehension of the whole, and of course conversely, we can focus on the whole only by diminishing our comprehension of the particulars which constitute the whole.

This Series is designed to present a kind of intellectual autobiography of each author, to portray the nature and meaning of the creative process for the creator and to show the relevance of his work to the feelings and aspirations of the man of flesh and bone. This Series endeavors to reflect also the influence of the work on the man and on society and to point to the freedom, or lack of freedom, to choose and pursue one profession rather than another.

It attempts to emphasize that the creator in any realm must surrender himself to a passionate pursuit of the hidden meaning of his labors, guided by deep personal intimations of an as yet undiscovered reality.

These volumes endeavor to indicate that it is impossible to know what constitutes a good society unless we know what defines a good individual. The self is determined by the values according to which it subordinates and integrates the rest of its values. If the values be transient, so is the self. If the values be dispersed and incoherent, so is the self. If they are organic and integrated, so is the self. The unity of human personality is its soundness. The unified self cannot be understood in terms of its constituent parts as dissected away from each other. So that finally what we see and what we do are no more and no less than what we are.

It is the effort of *The Credo Series* to define the new reality in which the estrangement of man and his work, resulting in the self-estrangement in man's existence, is overcome. This new reality is born through the reconciliation of what a man *knows* with what a man *is*. Being itself in all its presuppositions and implications can only be understood through the totality, through wholeness. St. Paul, who, like Isaiah before him, went into the market place not to secularize truth but to proclaim it, taught man that the "new creation" could be explained only by conquering the daemonic cleavages, the destructive split, in soul and cosmos. And that fragmentation always destroys a unity, produces a tearing away from the source and thereby creates disunity and isolation. The fruit can never be separated from the tree. The Tree of Life can never be disjoined from the Tree of Knowledge for both have *one and the same* root. And if man allows himself to fall into isolation, if he seeks to maintain a self segregated from the totality of which he is a necessary part, if he chooses to remain asunder, unrelated to the original context of all created things in which he too has his place—including his own labors—then this act of apostasy bears fruit in the demiurgical presumption of *magic*, a form of animism in which man seeks an authority of the self, placing himself above the law of the universe by attempting to separate the inseparable. He thus creates an unreal world of false contexts after having destroyed or deserted the real. And in this way the method of analysis, of scientific objectivity, which is good and necessary in its right place, is endowed with a destructive power when it is allowed to usurp a place for which it is not fitted.

The naturalist principle that man is the measure of all things has been shattered more than ever in our own age by the question, "What is the measure of man?" Post-modern man is more profoundly perplexed about the nature of man than his ancestors were. He is on the verge of spiritual and moral insanity. He does not know who he is. And having lost the sense of who and what he is, he fails to grasp the meaning of his fellow man, of his vocation, and of the nature and purpose of knowledge itself. For what is not understood cannot be known. And it is this cognitive faculty which is frequently abrogated by the "scientific" theory of knowledge, a theory that refuses to recognize the existence of comprehensive entities as distinct from their particulars. The central act of knowing is indeed that form of comprehension which is never absent from any process of knowing and is finally its ultimate sanction.

Science itself acknowledges as real a host of entities that cannot be described completely in materialistic or mechanistic terms, and it is this transcendence out of the domain of science into a region from which science itself can be appraised that *The Credo Series* hopes to expose. For the essence of the ebb and flow of experience, of sensations, the richness of the immediacy of directly apprehended knowledge, the metaphysical substance of what assails our being, is the very act itself of sensation and affection and therefore must escape the net of rational analysis, yet is intimately related to every cognitive act. It is this increasing intellectual climate that is calling into birth once more the compelling Socratic questions, "What is the purpose of life, the meaning of work?" "What is man?" Plato himself could give us only an indirect answer: "Man is declared to be that creature who is constantly in search of himself, a creature who at every moment of his existence must examine and scrutinize the conditions of his existence. He is a being in search of meaning."

Theory and life always go together. An organic conception of man and his work, man and society, man and the universe, is portrayed in First Corinthians 12 when Paul relates the famous story of the strife that once broke out between the parts of the human body. They refused to fulfill their special functions within the organism until they finally learned that they are all parts of one body and can exist and function only as such. For they all breathe together. And by so doing subordinate themselves to the presentation of the whole body. What may be an explanation of organic life in the human body may be transferred to the life in the universe and to the relationship between the interior and the exterior, for all is permeated by the life-giving creative power—by unity.

The authors in this endeavor are aware that man in the twentieth century finds himself in the greatest revolution since the discovery of agriculture. They show, each in his own way, that part of the meaning of our present turmoil may indeed lie in its being the means to reconcile thought and action, to overcome the parochialism of dogmas that only isolate man from man and man from the implicit meaning of his chosen profession. Our effort is to create an image of man intelligible and unitary, a microcosmic mirror of the greater macrocosm of which he is a part and in which he has his legitimate place in relation to the whole. For even the extraordinary successes of scientific predictions, the fruits of man's ingenuity in inventing the scientific method, seem comprehensible only on the basis that the human mind possesses an inherent logic closely parallel with the structure of the external world itself.

The very interdependence of the observer and the participant can no longer be ignored as part of the essential value of things. To take a definitive example from modern cosmology, it is challenging indeed to note that there is a most unusual connection between the existence of stars and the laws that govern the atomic nuclei. Emphasis is placed upon the existence, not the properties, of stars. For everyone expects the properties of stars and atomic nuclei to be related. It is the *connection* with the *existence* of stars that is so reassuring—and indeed surprising.

From this it is evident that there is present in the universe a *law* applicable to all nature including man and his work. Life itself then is seen to be a creative process elaborating and maintaining *order* out of the randomness of matter, endlessly generating new and unexpected structures and properties by building up associations that qualitatively transcend their constituent parts. This is not to diminish the importance of "scientific objectivity." It is, however, to say that the mind possesses a quality that cannot be isolated or known exclusively in the sense of objective knowledge. For it consists in that elusive humanity in us, our self, that knows. It is that inarticulate awareness that includes and *comprehends* all we know. It consists in the irreducible active voice of man and is recognized only in other things, only when the circle of consciousness closes around its universe of events.

The experience of the modern mind has been expressed in terms of conflict produced by false dualisms, disruption, self-destruction, meaninglessness, purposelessness and desperation. This character of our time has found its expression in literature, in art, in existential philosophy, in some forms of natural science, in political demonologies, and is explored in the psychology of the unconscious. Our authors hope to indicate that through a quickening of awareness man can overcome this dualism and can rise to face the meaning of life and work, keeping his mind and energies awake at full stretch. Such knowledge—that form of knowledge which cannot be disjoined from being—will enable man to embrace life with passion and to work with devotion. It will enable him to absorb experience with his whole nature and thereby to fill a want that is satisfied neither by action alone nor by thought alone. This unity of *being* and *doing* has a justifiable claim to be called a form of enchantment since through it men, who might otherwise give in to the malice of circumstances and conditions, find their old powers revived or new powers stirring within them, and through these life is sustained, renewed and fulfilled.

Man is now confronting himself with the compelling need to create an organic identification between what he *is* and what he *does*. For only in this way can the threat of conformism and the treachery of abstraction, the plight of the modern mind, be conquered. This split, inherited from the seventeenth century, between the transitive and the intransitive, between the creator and the process of creativity, has blunted man's appetite for experience. Language itself in our time has failed because man has forgotten that it is the mother of thought, because of its analytical emphasis and thus lacks ready means to convey associations, emotional or imaginative, that cluster around a subject and give to it a distinctive personal significance. In other words, the symbols by which man lives and has his being, that "tacit coefficient" * of articulate knowledge that is unanalyzable, now knocks at the portals of consciousness waiting to be admitted. For human nature loses its most precious quality when it is robbed of its sense of things beyond, unexplored and yet insistent.

The Credo Series belongs to those ideas that are intuitively conceived and that originate in spheres of a spiritual order and surprise thought, as it were, compelling it to transform its inherited notions conformably with its enlarged vision of the nature of things. It is as though the authors of the Series were recovering this reality out of a memory of a lost harmony, a memory latent in the soul and not distilled from the changing things of mere physical observation. In this way the inner unity of the known and the knower may be preserved, and the almost mythic intuition of reality thereby related to its conceptual and rational forms of expression. For man, unlike a machine, is an organism existing as an end in itself. He *is* the system on which causal explanations are based and to which they have to return; he *is* a historically existent whole, a four-dimensional entity, and not merely an abstraction from which statements about phenomena are deducible under the guise of eternity.

* See the classical work, *Personal Knowledge,* by Michael Polanyi for an enlarged meaning of the nature of reality. (Chicago University Press, 1958)

Our hope is to point to a new dimension of morality—not that of constraint and prohibition but a morality that lies as a fountainhead within the human soul, a morality of aspiration to spiritual experience. It suggests that necessity is laid upon us to infer entities that are not observed and are not observable. For an unseen universe is necessary to explain the seen. The flux is seen, but to account for its structure and its nature we infer particles of various kinds to serve as the vertices of the changing patterns, placing less emphasis on the isolated units and more on the structure and nature of relations. The process of knowing involves an immaterial becoming, an immaterial identification, and finally, knowledge itself is seen to be a dependent variable of immateriality. And somewhere along this spiritual pilgrimage man's pure observation is relinquished and gives way to the deeper experience of awe, for there can be no explanation of a phenomenon by searching for its origin but only by discerning its immanent law—this quality of transcendence that abides even in matter itself.

The present situation in the world and the vast accretion of knowledge have produced a serious anxiety, which may be overcome by re-evaluating the character, kinship, logic and operation of man in relation to his work. For work implies goals and intimately affects the person performing the work. Therefore the correlation and relatedness of ideas, facts and values that are in perpetual interplay could emerge from these volumes as they point to the inner synthesis and organic unity of man and his labors. For though no labor alone can enrich the person, no enrichment can be achieved without absorbing and intense labor. We then experience a unity of faith, labor and grace which prepares the mind for receiving a truth from sources over which it has no control. This is especially true since the great challenge of our age arises out of man's inventions in relation to his life.

Thus *The Credo Series* seeks to encourage the perfection not only of man's works but also and above all the fulfillment of himself as a person. And so we now are summoned to consider not only man in the process of development as a human subject but also his influence on the object of his investigation and creation. Observation alone is interference. The naïve view that we can observe any system and predict its behavior without altering it by the very act of observation was an unjustified extrapolation from Newton's *Celestial Mechanics*. We can observe the moon or even a satellite and predict its behavior without appreciably interfering with it, but we cannot do this with an amoeba, far less with a man and still less with a society of men. It is the heart of the question of the nature of work itself. If we regard our labors as a process of shaping or forming, then the fruits of our labors play the part of a mold by which we ourselves are shaped. And this means, in the preservation of the identity of the knower and the known, that cognition and generation, that is, creation, though in different spheres, are nevertheless alike.

It is hoped that the influence of such a Series may help to overcome the serious bifurcation of function and meaning and may show that the extraordinary crisis through which the world is passing can be fruitfully met by recognizing that knowledge has not been completely dehumanized and has not totally degenerated into a mere notebook over-crowded with formulas that few are able to understand or apply.

For mankind is now engaged in composing a new theme. Life refuses to be embalmed alive. Life cannot abjure life;

nothing that lives is born out of nothingness. But nothing, either, can preserve its form against the ceaseless flux of being. Life never manifests itself in negative terms. And our hope lies in drawing from every category of work a conviction that non-material values can be discovered in positive, affirmative, visible things. The estrangement between the temporal and non-temporal man is coming to an end, community is inviting communion and a vision of the human condition more worthy of man is engendered, connecting ever more closely the creative mind with the currents of spiritual energy which breaks for us the bonds of habit and keeps us in touch with the permanence of being in all its plenitude through our work.

And as, long ago, the Bearers of Bread were succeeded by the Bearers of Torches, so now, in the immediacies of life, it is the image of man and his vocation that can rekindle the high passion of humanity in its quest for light. Refusing to divorce work from life or love from knowledge, it is action, it is passion that enhances our being.

We live in an expanding universe and also in the moral infinite of that other universe, the universe of man. And along the whole stretched arc of this universe we may see that extreme limit of complicity where reality seems to shape itself within the work man has chosen for his realization. Work then becomes not only a way of knowledge, it becomes even more a way of life—of life in its totality. For the last end of every maker is himself.

"And the places that have been desolate for ages shall be built in thee: thou shalt raise up the foundations of generation and generation; and thou shalt be called the repairer of the fences, turning the paths into rest." *

—RUTH NANDA ANSHEN

* Isaiah, 58:12

OLD WINE, NEW BOTTLES:
A Humanist Teacher at Work

I
THE ESSENTIAL ENTERPRISE

I AM a teacher. Except for wars and holidays I have never been out of the sound of a school bell. I have written books and given public lectures, but these I have regarded as part of my teaching. The life I lead is the most agreeable I can imagine. I go from my study to a classroom well lighted, comfortably heated, with clean blackboards and fresh chalk, where there await me a group of intelligent and curious young men who read the books assigned them with a sense of adventure and discovery, discuss them with zest, and listen appreciatively to explications I may offer. What makes the process most satisfying is the conviction that what goes on in my own and a thousand other classrooms is more important than the large affairs carried on in the shining palaces of aluminum and glass downtown. For I believe that education is mankind's most important enterprise.

Everything that raises man above the rest of animal creation he must learn. Elemental survival requires expertness which must be taught, and survival at a level which men regard tolerable requires many kinds of specialized expertness. It is obvious that we need people who understand the production of food, and nearly as obvious that we need people who understand electronics. It is no less obvious (though its very obviousness may blind us to the fact) that oncoming members of the human society need to be initiated into its outlooks and habits of thought and cultural symbols.

That the expertness requisite for elemental survival must be fostered and propagated no generation since Cain and Abel has ever doubted, nor has there been significant opposition to mankind's incessant drive for abundance and comfort beyond elemental needs. Misgivings there have been. When Prometheus brought fire to man, according to the ancient legend, and so facilitated his rapid progress in arts and crafts, Zeus was angry; presumably, modern moralists have suggested, because the exploitation of fire must eventually lead to something like a hydrogen bomb. But in themselves increments to physical well-being have never obstructed, but have rather promoted, the total well-being of mankind. Concern for spiritual values does not require rejection of material conveniences which technological progress makes available.

What the moralist's suspicion of material progress is based upon, ultimately, is the inveterate notion that body and soul are more or less disparate entities, so that attention to one must imply neglect of the other. The origin of this dualism of body and soul, at least in the western tradition, is in the teaching of the Orphics; among the classical Greeks its foremost spokesman is Plato; from whatever source it was derived, it has long been part of all the religious orthodoxies known to Europe. A phrase attributed to Orpheus speaks of the body (*soma*) as being the tomb (*sema*) of the soul; what man must do is to suppress the demands of the body, so far as he can, and so liberate the soul from its trammels.

Carried to its extreme, as among Neoplatonists and religious ascetics, this doctrine led to an utter contempt of the body. Whereas in the anthropocentric Greek view a man's excellence was measured by the degree to which he realized his human potentialities, in this view he was considered excellent in the degree that he put off his humanity and assimilated himself to an ideal outside man. The world of the senses is illusory, and transitory life in this unreal world is only a prelude to a fuller life in the real and abiding world. Preoccupation with the goods of this ephemeral world is therefore not only futile but a positive hindrance to the true good.

So absolute a division between body and soul was doubtless held by only a minority in classical antiquity, nor has it been the sole, perhaps not even the dominant, view in the modern world. But even among those who do not fully subscribe to it the view continues effective, if only as a metaphor. Whether or not we associate material interests and spiritual interests with disparate entities in the human composition, we do tend to think of them as belonging to separate categories. And since our total capacities are limited, with the material and spiritual ideally in balance, any weight added to the scale of the material must diminish the scale of the spiritual.

The metaphor is inescapable because of the ambiguity inherent in the word "spiritual." If "spirit" is equivalent to "soul" and hence an independent entity (as it apparently is in Matthew's "the spirit is willing but the flesh is weak"), then the adjective "spiritual" must refer specifically to soul, and "spiritual" education is immeasurably more important than any other kind. In ordinary usage, however, we apply "spiritual" to the various intellectual and emotional and aesthetic interests of man which we need not believe detachable from his physical organism, because we have no other word so convenient. This is the sense in which I shall use "spiritual" in this little book; even in this sense, as I shall try to show, spiritual education is at least as important as any other.

Actually the imprecise adjective is correct in this context because the conception it describes is ambiguous. There can be no exact and universally acceptable definition of what nonmaterial elements must be included in the educational process, nor can there be agreement, even in an element universally acceptable, on the weight of emphasis it should receive and on what aspects should be favored or deprecated. If men differ on the desirability of types of food or fabrics, recourse can be had to objective tests to determine which is the more wholesome, and reasonable people will willingly accept the decision. But laboratory tests cannot decide between varying opinions on the style in which the food should be served or the fabric trimmed. Perhaps it is because criteria of taste cannot be established on objective grounds that individual positions are held the more stubbornly and defended more ardently. Where weights and measures are equivocal it is natural that emotional voltage should be brought into play. So for the material aspects of education, in which the goals are definable, decisions on desirable proportions and procedures can be reached by the impersonal logic of measuring devices and efficiency ratings. But in the realm of spiritual education even those who acquiesce in its general desirability differ widely on the question of goals, and even more widely on questions of proportions and procedures, and there is no objective criterion by which differences can be reconciled. Each partisan is guided by his own convictions and commitments, and his only means for winning his opponents over is eloquence based upon an appeal to the emotions. Where logic cannot serve, something like a credo must take its place.

Except as a noun signifying the traditional formulation of a creed or the musical setting for it, *credo* is an uncomfortable word on modern lips. What it brings to mind is something like the affirmation attributed to Tertullian, *credo quia absurdum est,* "I believe because it is absurd." To base conviction on illogicality marks a man a fool in the eyes of the sober; to claim (as the emphatic *I* seems to do) that he is superior to other men marks him a sanctimonious fraud; and the endeavor to persuade other men to his folly (as the public profession implies) marks him a fanatic. Where "credo" does occur in contemporary speech, its overtones are apt to be vulgar ("our credo is 'the customer is right' "), or cynical ("my credo is 'take the cash and let the credit go' "), and in any case materialistic. "The substance of things hoped for, the evidence of things not seen" leaves a modern generation puzzled if not suspicious. We sophisticates have learned to demand tangi-

ble demonstration and to distrust persuasion: if the per-
suader is not bent upon negotiable profit, he must be
seeking to reassure himself of the validity of a questionable
position by seeing others accept it.

If there is one area of secular activity in which "credo"
is not too pretentious a word, in which it can be used
without cynicism or vulgarity, that area is the education
I have called spiritual, for such education does, in fact,
and for the secular it alone does, subsume and represent
the nonmaterial concerns of mankind. It is the one area
in which the man who professes a credo may well risk
being dismissed as fool, fraud, or fanatic, and in which the
light he may hope to shed is worth the candle.

For most of the centuries of European history qualify-
ing education as spiritual would be as tautological as calling water wet. It is still so for what I am pleased to think
is the more thoughtful fraction of civilized humanity, and
the inherited weight of this view is such that people who
may inwardly doubt its validity still pay formal obeisance
to it—as people may do who do not inwardly accept the
premises of organized religion. But if we were to tabulate
our various institutions concerned with the transmission of
knowledge and the offerings and enrollments in *all* educational institutions, I suspect that the qualifications of a
certain kind of education as spiritual would not be otiose.

It is this kind of education that I personally have been
concerned with all the working years of my life. My
conviction that communicating the spiritual legacy of the
race is an essential function for civilized men is, of course,

very widely shared. With another view which I hold almost as firmly, however, I should expect to find far less agreement, that is, that the most effective and economical way for communicating the legacy is through the study of the body of literature we call the classics. It is mainly to advocate this view, on the basis of traditional educational practice and of my own experiences, that I write these pages. I propose to say how teaching of the body of knowledge I am concerned with has been regarded and has been carried on in the past, and what I conceive the function of its teachers to be today. I shall have to touch upon some areas of history and to offer some definitions, but I must insist that this essay is not a textbook and that it makes no pretense of objectivity. By prescription of the editor of the series of which it is a part, it is personal and hence subjective; what I write is not an accepted consensus but the thoughts I have had, in the course of my experience, on what my own professions signify.

It may be said, indeed, that my zeal for a particular kind of education is motivated by profit, for it is the education by which I have gained my livelihood, and by the need for reassurance, for it is the kind of education which is now on the defensive. No man is wholly altruistic and none can know to what degree his attitudes are shaped by self-interest; but so far as I am aware, my special pleading is untainted. As to the profit motive, I can only say that I am so near retirement that if the pursuits I live by and advocate were suddenly abolished my livelihood would not be imperilled.

Nor am I in need of reassurance. Not only in school and college but even in graduate school I studied the ancient languages and literatures simply because I thought they were interesting and important subjects, with no thought of making a professional career of teaching them. I was prepared to enter a different career, which was likely to prove more remunerative, when I was invited, quite unexpectedly, to join the department of which I am still a member. I accepted with alacrity, but with some regret that I had lost my amateur standing: what I had done out of love I was now doing for gain. I was relieved to find that the bursar would send my monthly salary directly to my bank, so that I could fancy that I was still doing what I wished to do out of love, and that some benignant power made it possible for me to draw checks for my food and shelter.

I still do not know what my university's pay checks look like. On two or three occasions in the intervening years other and quite satisfactory ways of life were open to me, but it has never occurred to me to take a path different from the one I have followed. And if all this is a veteran's arrogance or a weakling's whistling in the dark, there are so many and such considerable people who have no vested interest in my position and yet share it that I cannot feel isolated and in need of support.

II
WHAT ARE HUMANITIES?

THE KIND of subject matter and, more important, the approach to various kinds of subject matter that constitute my credo and that I wish to speak for, are associated with the term "Humanities." The general intent of the term is clear enough, but it is susceptible to various interpretations and emphases; my first task must therefore be to clarify its meaning, and this can best be done by considering its history.

As a designation for particular academic subject matter and approach "Humanities" is not an ancient word; it first came into use in the late medieval universities in Italy, and has received new currency, with slightly altered significance, only within the last twenty-five years. Traditionally the universities were organized by faculties, as of law, of medicine, of theology. A student who was not associated with these faculties but who wished to devote himself to language and literature instead was said to pursue *studia humaniora* or *studia humanitatis,* or, in English, Humanities. The only languages and literatures deemed worthy of serious study were, of course, those of Greece and Rome.

Implicit in the conception of Humanities, then, are two

11

principles of central importance. First, the Humanities are
nonprofessional. For studies properly to be designated
Humanities it is essential that they must not contribute,
except incidentally or by indirection, to training for a
professional career. This qualification still obtains. Second,
the immediate association of "Humanities" is with the
languages and literatures of Greece and Rome. Initially the
monopoly of the classics was not a matter of arbitrary
choice or of snobbery; there were in fact no other secular
literatures that were artistic and mature available for
study. But even after vernacular literatures arose to challenge the monopoly of the ancients, the term Humanities
retained its special association with the classics. So European schools called Humanistic are those which teach
quantities of Greek and Latin, and the man in charge of
Latin studies in a Scottish university is Professor of
Humanity.

The title is, of course, quaint, and only a conscious
archaizer would today speak of the study of Greek and
Latin as the Humanities. But since World War II the word
has received new currency in American colleges, to desig-
nate comprehensive courses in great books and in masterpieces of music and the fine arts. The contents of current
Humanities courses are naturally not the same as the
curriculum of *Humanistisches Gymnasium* or the program
of a Scottish Professor of Humanities, but they do retain
something of the two essentials characteristic of their
origin: they are nonprofessional, and they are largely
concerned with classical antiquity. The course called
Humanities in my own college includes representative
books from Homer to the nineteenth century, yet fully half

of the works studied are translations from Greek or Latin.

It is worth while to notice how and why the thing now called Humanities and its name came into use. The distinctive feature of higher education in America has always been the College of Liberal Arts, with the adjective "Liberal" consciously set in emphatic opposition to "practical." Visitors from abroad were often astonished to find that young men who had no intention of entering a learned profession, but who looked forward to careers in agriculture or commerce or industry, would nevertheless devote themselves seriously to philosophy and literature. There can be no doubt that the tradition of the Liberal Arts colleges has contributed substantially to shaping our national character and outlooks.

But then new kinds of knowledge began to make insistent and not unreasonable demands upon the attention of educated man. And as the organization and appurtenances of life became more and more complex, even the layman required more and more expert knowledge to confront it intelligently. The new kinds of knowledge and expertise demanded an increasing share of the student's time. The study of the ancient languages had always been in the nature of a luxury; now it began to be looked upon as conspicuous waste. The luxury had been regarded as appropriate for the relatively small elect who could afford the privilege of higher education; as higher education became more widespread, the validity of the luxury came to be looked at more narrowly. It may be that the old teaching had been misdirected and uneconomical, and it may be that the new was overconfident and grasping; but whatever their imbalances, the new directions were as inevitable as they were essentially desirable. The most ardent devotee of Greek and Latin would not today insist that all students be required to study the ancient languages, or indeed that such students as do devote themselves to these languages should neglect other studies. None would send his son or daughter to a college which ignored modern physics or politics.

Though the old Liberal Arts program was curtailed, the ideal naturally survived. But when the composition of the curriculum was modified, it was found desirable to distinguish the subject matter and approach which had been central in the old Liberal Arts program from the newer and more specialized disciplines and approaches. The new designation for what had been nearly the whole of the old Liberal Arts program is General Education. General Education, as distinguished from the specialized education which is carried on simultaneously in the same institutions, is placed in the beginning years of the college course and is usually organized according to three large areas—the natural sciences, the political sciences, and a group including literature, philosophy, fine arts, and music. It should be said at once that no teacher of these courses, no matter how deeply he might be committed to them, would be satisfied that his students were being properly educated if he did not know that they were concurrently being subjected to the more rigorous disciplines of specialized education.

Put most succinctly, the difference between the two kinds of approach is this: whereas the teacher of a specialized course proceeds on the assumption that his students are all embryo chemists or economists or philologers, the teacher of a General Educaton course knows that he is

addressing amateurs and seeks to assist them to the widest
and fullest possible understanding of their physical and
social and intellectual environment. Least successful in the
General Education group are the courses in natural
science, perhaps because the student must in fact go
through an actual apprenticeship, including long hours in
the laboratory, to understand the scientist's work. General
Education courses in the social sciences, frequently called
Contemporary Civilization, do succeed in organizing history and anthropology, politics and economics, so that the
layman is enlightened but also sufficiently informed to
proceed to specialized work in one of the component disciplines that may attract him.

Hardest to define, in content and objective, is the third
group, frequently called Humanities, which is the principal
heir and continuator of the Liberal Arts tradition. The
design of Humanities courses, in general terms, is to initiate the young, as fully as may be, into the intellectual
and artistic legacy of the race, in order to inform and
enrich their sensibilities as laymen, not to prepare them
for professional work in a given field. The latter point is
important. Teachers of the Humanities should themselves
be professional scholars with specialties of their own, and
should also be giving specialized courses. But a professional scholar training new members of his guild is not
engaged in teaching the Humanities even if his subject is
Greek. The approach is as important a condition as the
subject matter; Greek is not necessarily a Humanity, in
the Liberal Arts sense, and natural science may and indeed
should be.

Is it enough for a subject to be nonpractical for it to be

called a Humanity? In institutions where the practical is dominant anything "cultural" is classed with the Humanities; I have seen a college catalogue which lists a course in basket-weaving under Humanities. If the students are blind men learning to weave baskets to sell, the classification is obviously wrong; but what if their interest is solely aesthetic? There are two objections to calling such activities as basket-weaving Humanities. The lesser and more obvious objection is that they are not rich enough, as books are, to tell us much about the spiritual experiences and outlooks of the race.

But there is a more decisive objection, inherent in the fundamental conception of Humanities. Human culture is, as it were, a continuous texture rolling endlessly off a loom, with colors and patterns growing sometimes richer and more vivid, sometimes fading to drabness, sometimes recalling older patterns, sometimes developing new. What is expected of study of the Humanities is that they familiarize us with antecedent stretches of the work, so that we have a basis for evaluating and perhaps shaping new patterns. Our culture is too complicated a thing to be assimilated at a glance by a baby or a newcomer from Mars. The primary object of academic education is therefore to gather up, organize, and make meaningful the past experiences of the race.

An academic department of fine arts, for example, is mainly concerned with the history of the fine arts. It is, of course, useful for a practising artist to know what problems his predecessors confronted and how they solved them, and it is good for a historian of art to know how the contemporary practising artist attacks current problems;

but the practical technique of painting and sculpture is not an academic enterprise. The same applies to departments of literature. Teachers of English do have to drill awkward squads in the techniques of spelling and punctuation, and, at a more advanced level, teach what is optimistically called "creative writing." But their real business is with the content of the literary legacy of the past and with how and why it came to be what it is. This was more clearly understood a generation or two ago, perhaps, when only writers who had been dead long enough for their work to be seen in perspective received the attention of the academicians. Even in the mechanic arts it is enlightening and it may be useful for the practitioner to know the traditions of his mystery; in the humanistic arts the tradition is his main concern.

The teacher of the Humanities, in a word, is the curator of the spiritual legacy of the race, which it is his duty to cultivate and propagate. In his capacity as scholar he must strive to attain a fuller and purer understanding of his charge; in his capacity as teacher he must see that the legacy is communicated, in the greatest possible fullness and purity, to the largest possible number of the legitimate heirs of the legacy. Each exercises his curatorship according to his own capacities and inclinations. Some linger in their studies to add to and refine our knowledge of the past, some seek to interpret the knowledge, some to make it accessible through popularizations and translations, most to spread it abroad in classrooms. All of these functions are necessary for the proper curatorship of the legacy, and even those whose particular gifts lie in one kind of service participate in the others also.

An important item in the humanistic legacy, almost on a level with literature and philosophy and art, is the experience of the race in the care of it. Indeed, educational ideals can serve as a representative and manageable sample of the totality of spiritual ideals. It is worth while, therefore, to see how our predecessors conceived the duty of curatorship and how they discharged their duty.

III
GREEK PARADIGMS

At various classicizing periods in the history of European culture, enthusiastic admirers of Greek antiquity, themselves essentially romantic in temper, have sought to revive some Greek institution or outlook, whether in architecture or literature or costume, in an alien environment which the Greek originators of the pattern could themselves never have envisaged. The results have often been ludicrous and always stultifying—like the efforts of nineteenth-century Greek intellectuals, after their country attained independence, to "purify" their language of its natural transformations and accretions and restore it to its ancient norms. Literal copies of the modes of antiquity, in education as in other aspects of cultural life, must be as artificial as they were anachronistic.

And yet for apprehending the history of any European institution or outlook, it remains true that the most economical procedure is to look at its Greek origins. The Greeks were themselves heirs to antecedent traditions, whose various strands can be discerned in the skein of their own culture, but more than any other people we know they seem to have come fresh into their world, with intellectual power mature and alert but still untrammeled. Never, in the subsequent history of Europe, have men seemed so unconstrained in shaping or adapting their institutions. For us, then, the prime usefulness of the Greek paradigm is not as a model to copy but as a gauge to assess our own constructions.

Our literature and philosophy, our canons of taste, our conceptions of the proper relationships between man and man and between the individual and external authority, our views of the good life and our aspirations, are built, however high they have reached, upon Greek foundations. Examination of these foundations enables us to see, readily and surely, where and to what degree the superimposed storeys deviate from the plumb and to assess the serviceability of these deviations. They are not, of course, to be rejected out of hand simply because they are deviations, but we can judge whether they are mere aberrations, whether they are responses to emerging challenges, and whether they are adequate responses.

If the Greek experience does provide a paradigm, moreover, it is no single or exclusive one. Disparate religious, philosophical, and political outlooks flourished concurrently; there was no orthodoxy, and hence nothing could be branded heterodox. The romantic classicists who seize upon the single aspect that attracts them to copy are as wrong in their premises as in their conclusions; it is its fluidity that makes the study of the Greek experience profitable. A modern in search of guidance can follow the Platonists, if his inclination so moves him, or else the rationalist Sophists; but most useful of all, whichever his propensity or environment may have conditioned him to, the Greek experience can provide guidance for mobility from one to the other. Platonism, for example, was a factor in leading St. Augustine from paganism to Christianity, and sophistic thought a factor in leading certain Renaissance figures away from Augustinianism. The same fluidity and suggestiveness characterizes other aspects of Greek intellectual life, among them education. What makes the Greek experience in education useful to us, in the last analysis, are not details of organization or curriculum or of public versus private support, but the fact that their range of premises and objectives in education, as in political outlooks, was so like our own.

The Greeks not only practised education at various levels, as they obviously must have done, but speculated about it and, as we shall see, advocated strongly partisan positions. The major issue was between the professional and amateur attitudes even in the subjects we have called "spiritual," but before we examine that conflict a word must be said about the perennial opposition between cultural and technological education as it manifested itself among the Greeks. The procedures in the latter branches we can only surmise, for the books that have come down to us were written by literary men, not artisans, and show an upper-class bias. The kind of "gentleman's education" which Plato advocated (a passage on the subject will be quoted presently) he says is limited to those who can afford it and is directed by the parents. Aristotle says that "education should be regulated by law and should be a concern of the state," but he too draws a sharp distinction

between technical and cultural subjects. Here is his
rationale and something of his program (*Politics* 1337b):

> There can be no doubt that children should be taught
> those useful things which are really necessary, but not
> all useful things; for occupations are divided into liberal
> and illiberal; and to young children should be imparted
> only such kinds of knowledge as will be useful to them
> without vulgarizing them. And any occupation, art, or
> science, which makes the body or soul or mind of the
> freeman less fit for the practice or exercise of virtue, is
> vulgar; wherefore we call those arts vulgar which tend to
> deform the body, and likewise all paid employments, for
> they absorb and degrade the mind. There are also some
> liberal arts quite proper for a freeman to acquire, but
> only in a certain degree, and if he attend to them too
> closely, in order to attain perfection in them, the same
> evil effects will follow. The object also which a man sets
> before him makes a great difference; if he does or learns
> anything for his own sake or for the sake of his friends,
> or with a view to excellence, the action will not appear
> illiberal; but if done for the sake of others, the very same
> action will be thought menial and servile. The received
> subjects of instruction, as I have already remarked, are
> partly of a liberal and partly of an illiberal character.
>
> The customary branches of education are in number
> four; they are—(1) reading and writing, (2) gymnastic
> exercises, (3) music, to which is sometimes added (4)
> drawing. Of these, reading and writing and drawing are
> regarded as useful for the purposes of life in a variety of
> ways, and gymnastic exercises are thought to infuse
> courage. Concerning music a doubt may be raised—in

our days most men cultivate it for the sake of pleasure, but originally it was included in education, because nature herself, as has often been said, requires that we should be able not only to work well but to use leisure well; for as I must repeat once again, the first principle of all action is leisure.

Banausoi, the word for "craftsmen," Aristotle defines as "mechanics who practise the arts without which a city cannot exist." Elsewhere in the same treatise on *Politics* he says that "the best form of state will not admit them to citizenship." The *banausic* life he speaks of with great disparagement, and the adjective comes to signify "vulgar, in bad taste." In subsequent history, upper-class disdain of the *banausic* was more pronounced and the prestige of "cultural" education was more enhanced. In later antiquity, such education was even thought to confer special privileges upon its possessor in a future existence. The special prestige which attaches to a man who does not have to use his hands in his work still survives in the British usage of calling a physician "Doctor" and a surgeon "Mr." Here, it is interesting to observe, Aristotle himself was a revolutionary. Not the least of his contributions in the study of biology was the demonstration that it could be proper for a gentleman to roll his sleeves up and dissect a fish.

That artisans were carefully and efficiently trained we can be certain. Plato habitually speaks of the trades (which he of course disparages) as requiring a high degree of specialization, and the physical monuments of antiquity provide irrefutable evidence of high competence which

must be the result of a tradition of expertness long culti-
vated and carefully transmitted. Modern metallurgists
marvel at the skill with which Greek sculptors alloyed their
metals and cast their bronze figures—of which Praxiteles
alone is said to have fabricated fifteen hundred. The subtle
refinements with which the architects of the Parthenon
introduced curves and varied spacing of columns to correct
optical distortions bespeak a sophistication in theory and
a skill in execution which have never been surpassed. And
so it is with the so-called minor arts also.

The line between artisan and artist is ambiguous and
differently placed at different times. The great architects
and painters and sculptors were obviously highly respected,
for their names are recorded and were as familiar in antiquity as the names of the great literary artists. If competence in the arts were not esteemed, potters would not
have taken pains to sign their productions. Plutarch
records that Phidias, the sculptor who designed the statu-
ary and reliefs for the Parthenon, was on terms of intimacy
with Pericles, who was the most eminent Athenian of his
time. And yet in the same *Life of Pericles* Plutarch remarks that no father, however much he admired the work
of a sculptor or a musician, would wish his son to follow
their trades. Plutarch's attitude may in part reflect his
consistent loyalty to Plato, and in greater part the much
lower esteem in which artists (at least living ones) were
held in the Roman world.

If *banausic* employment lowered a man's social status,
it did not permanently relegate him to an inferior class.
We know of a number of individuals who rose to higher
station through special ability; Socrates was the son of a

stonecutter, and the demagogues who succeeded Pericles, if we can trust Aristophanes' pasquinades, were sausage sellers and tanners. Education for the learned professions was carried on in regular schools or guilds. The most famous was the school of medicine associated with the name of Hippocrates on the island of Cos. The tradition of epic poetry appears to have been something of a monopoly in a guild called the *Homeridae,* and the reciters of epic poetry called *rhapsodes* insisted on their professional standing. At a later period actors were members of an association of artists of Dionysus, which presumably insisted on competent preparation. The writing of speeches for cases at law was recognized as a profession which was taught by experts, but here we know of people who applied their amateur knowledge to professional use for financial need—like the man of our earlier example who studied basket-weaving for aesthetic satisfaction, and then fell blind and made a livelihood of his art, or like a man who learns Greek for fun and then finds he can get his bread by it.

On what we have called "spiritual" education we are much better informed. Beginning with Homer, who tells us that Phoenix was charged with making his pupil Achilles "a speaker of words and a doer of deeds," we sense in a number of authors the unremitting effort to inculcate the ideals of the group into those who would become part of it. All of adult society was thought to be in a kind of conspiracy to achieve this aim; in Sparta citizens were as responsible for admonishing and chastening their neighbors' children as they were for their own. It was the requirement to maintain the ideals of the group which enabled the Greeks to Hellenize the easterners among whom they settled in the Hellenistic age instead of being submerged by them. And it was the sense of the group ideal, which came to be transformed into a kind of cult, which enabled Hellenism to survive under Roman domination. A good summary of the process of "spiritual" education and its objectives is a statement put into the mouth of the sophist Protagoras (who was in Athens in the middle of the fifth century B.C.) in Plato's dialogue called after his name:

Education and admonition commence in the first years of childhood, and last to the very end of life. Mother and nurse and father and tutor are vying with one another about the improvement of the child as soon as ever he is able to understand what is being said to him: he cannot say or do anything without their setting forth to him that this is just and that is unjust; this is honorable, that is dishonorable; this is holy, that is unholy; do this and abstain from that. And if he obeys, well and good; if not, he is straightened by threats and blows, like a piece of bent or warped wood. At a later stage they send him to teachers, and enjoin them to see to his manners even more than to his reading and music; and the teachers do as they are desired. And when the boy has learned his letters and is beginning to understand what is written, as before he understood only what was spoken, they put into his hands the works of great poets, which he reads sitting on a bench at school; in these are contained many admonitions, and many tales, and praises, and encomia of ancient famous men, which he is required to learn by heart, in order that he may imitate or emulate them and desire to become like them. Then, again, the teachers of the lyre take similar care that their young disciple is temperate and gets into no mischief; and when they have taught him the use of the lyre, they introduce him to the poems of other excellent poets, who are the lyric poets; and these they set to music, and make their harmonies and rhythms quite familiar to the children's souls, in order that they may learn to be more gentle and harmonious, and rhythmical, and so more fitted for speech and action; for the life of man in every part has need of harmony and rhythm. Then they send him to the master of gymnastic, in order that their bodies may better minister to the virtuous mind, and that they may not be compelled through bodily weakness to play the coward in war or on any other occasion. This is what is done by those who have the means, and those who have the means are the rich; their children begin to go to school soonest and leave off latest. When they have done with masters, the state again compels them to learn the laws, and live after the pattern which they furnish, and not after their own fancies; and just as in learning to write, the writing-master first draws lines with a stylus for the use of the young beginner, and gives him the tablet and makes him follow the lines, so the

city draws the laws, which were the invention of good
lawgivers living in the olden time; these are given to
the young man, in order to guide him in his conduct
whether he is commanding or obeying; and he who
transgresses them is to be corrected.

The objective of the educational process here described
is what recruiting officials for colleges nowadays call "the
well-rounded man"; the term is useful enough, though the
image it evokes is unfortunate, and the distortions and
dilutions perpetrated in its name make people like myself
wince. If gymnastics are provided for, to make the body a
fit instrument for the strenuous demands that might be
made upon it, the ultimate objective, it must be noticed, is
"that their bodies may better minister to the virtuous
mind." *Gymnastike* and *mousike* (which includes literature as well as music) are the regular components of
Greek education, but *mousike* always has the place of
honor. For us the most striking statement in the *Protagoras*
passage, presented apparently as a truism, is that the object of education is to make men's lives gentle and harmonious and rhythmical. For this purpose the proper
instrument is stated to be "poetry" (which includes all
creative writing), and elsewhere in the *Protagoras* we are
shown how a detailed explication of a poem of Simonides
might be made the basis for a penetrating discussion of
ethics and good citizenship.

Protagoras himself is rather roughly handled by his
junior Socrates in Plato's dialogue. Protagoras, who was a
highly respected and much sought-after teacher, claims

that virtue can be taught; Socrates (who is the spokesman for Plato's own convictions) insists that specific accomplishments can indeed be taught, but that virtue cannot be. In the end the disputants seem to reverse their positions, with Socrates insisting that only virtue can be taught and Protagoras maintaining that it cannot be. The inconsistencies are more apparent than real, because both "virtue" and "teaching" undergo subtle shifts in meaning in the course of the argument. Expounders have clarified the course of the discussion in several ways: one easy and adequate explanation is that Plato, here as elsewhere, holds that education must be specialized and professional whereas Protagoras holds that it must be general and amateur. Plato's views on the subject are apparent in many parts of his writings, especially in the *Republic,* and were actualized in the Academy which he established. Protagoras' views are in the sophist tradition, of which he was himself the outstanding exponent, and were actualized in the school which Isocrates established. The issue is one of prime and abiding importance, and its essentials and implications are crystallized in the views and careers of the two men. We must therefore look at the practices and aims of the two schools more narrowly.

IV

PROFESSIONAL AND AMATEUR

THE earliest European institutions recognizably analogous to our own colleges are two established in Athens early in the fourth century, one by Plato, and the other by Isocrates. Neither made startling innovations in the organization and methods of education; rather, out of the practices already existing each selected and regularized elements suitable for his own purposes. What is more important in their achievement is the discovery and crystallization of the main categories of education, in content and approach. Plato called his subject matter philosophy, and Isocrates called his oratory, but the difference between the two schools went much further than their ostensible subject matter. In view of the towering position which Plato occupies in the history of western thought and of the prestige which attaches to the word philosophy, it might be supposed that his was the school which affected subsequent educational theory most powerfully: actually it was Isocrates' program which prevailed —and happily so for the course of our culture. We must see where the real issue between the two lay.

To appreciate Plato's position, it is well to know something of his political outlook. Plato was descended from the ancient nobility and his associations were aristocratic. Specifically, his kinsmen and friends Critias and Charmides were leaders in the tyranny of the Thirty which arrogated power to itself in 404 B.C. when Athens was sinking to its fall and which tried to maintain its power by a ruthless program of assassination and confiscation. The tyranny was suppressed by an armed democratic reaction, but loathing for its members persisted; and the fact that some of its leading figures had been "companions" of Socrates surely contributed to the condemnation of Socrates in 399. It was the political immorality he had experienced in his twenties and the death of Socrates, "the best and wisest man he had ever known," that turned Plato from the political career upon which he had embarked to the study and teaching of philosophy. Until philosophers should become kings or kings philosophers, he believed states would never be well-governed.

We shall notice that the salient characteristics of Plato's educational scheme are that it is authoritarian, that it is exclusive, and that it is specialist, the latter two traits being functions of the first. All three are implicit in Plato's political theory which his educational program is designed to promote. The education and the regimen which Plato envisages under his philosopher-king is not calculated to please a democratic temper. The state will doubtless be orderly and its citizens disciplined, but all individualism will be discouraged. A man must occupy the station in life and follow the calling assigned to him, he cannot marry as he chooses or lead a family life, he can read only what books survive a censorship which will abolish literature that may foster individualism. The ultimate objec-

tive of this education is, indeed, to raise its beneficiaries
to a higher ideal, of which the outlines, however, remain
vague and depend largely upon the authority of the master.

The authority of the philosophic ruler, and equally of
the teacher, rests upon a claim to special and unique insights, and we must look at the background and implications of this claim. Plato is a very great artist, but his most
masterly and enduring creation is the image of Socrates.
Most of the dialogues in which Socrates figures, and especially those dealing with his trial and death and the
Symposium, have, as at least a collateral purpose, the de-
piction of Socrates as a saintly personage with insights
not shared by other men. Socrates must indeed have been
an extraordinary man, but the special aura which sur-
rounds him is surely Plato's creation, for the Socrates of
Xenophon (to say nothing of the caricature in Aristophanes' *Clouds*) has nothing of the exalted quality of
Plato's. For the specially endowed teacher who spoke with
authority not vouchsafed to ordinary men, there was prec-
edent in Greek tradition: Orpheus, Empedocles, and especially Pythagoras (all of whom may have been shamans
or may have derived from shamanism) spoke as with
supernatural authority. We may note that Plato's image
of Socrates, including his heroic death, became in turn a
model for the *aretalogies* or "sacred biographies" of later
teachers whose successors, honest men or charlatans, used
them as a kind of scripture to give authority to their
teachings.

We can now understand why Plato himself insists, in

his autobiographical *Seventh Epistle,* that his doctrine cannot be learned from his books (which were of course accessible to anyone who could purchase them) but must be communicated, after long personal association, as by a spark from master to disciple. Such a requirement is sufficient evidence of the exclusiveness of Plato's educational program, particularly in comparison with the system of the Isocratean school, which trusted books and trusted people to use them. The authoritarian view naturally implies specialization, and Plato's conviction in this respect may be seen in his repeated statements of the absurdity of the flautist undertaking to train horses, and vice versa, and of the utter absurdity of allowing either a vote in matters on which only the statesman has competence. The teacher himself, in other words, is a professional, and his disciples, whatever their careers, must be only professionals. For intellectual discipline Plato favored mathematics, and the principal occupation in the Academy seems in fact to have been the study of mathematics.

Before proceeding to consider the Isocratean system, we may pause to see how the Platonic was carried on. Aristotle remained in the Academy for twenty years, but the spark apparently never kindled, for he then went off to found his own school. But though the Lyceum diverged from the Academy in essential ways, in the matter of educational practice it carried Plato's theory to an extreme. What the Lyceum or the Peripatetic school amounted to was highly specialized seminar and laboratory work in a series of scholarly subjects. The results, whether in politics or biology, in literary criticism or biography, showed the highest technical proficiency, but the scholarship was insulated from a larger public—as it would be again in the nineteenth century.

As a philosophical school in the proper sense the Peripatetics went into oblivion two or three generations after Aristotle, and its philosophic teachings were revived only in the Roman period. But its scholarly procedures, in natural science and in philology, were carried forward in the Museum endowed by the Ptolemies in Alexandria. It was only in modern times that the scholarly devotion and acumen of the Alexandrians have been equalled, but their work was even more insulated from the larger public. The effect of exclusively professional ideals becomes apparent in cultural life as a whole. In the classical period a well-bred man was expected to perform gracefully in the gymnasium; now he must be a champion. He was able to accompany himself on a musical instrument; now he must be a virtuoso. He was expected to read and have opinions about books; now he must be a philologist.

The education which Isocrates favored did not compartmentalize learning and did not aim to produce specialists. His program was oratory or, more properly, discourse, and though many of his pupils did in fact become orators, as many became historians or statesmen, so that his school cannot be looked upon as a specialist institution preparing candidates for a profession. Oratory, as moderns understand the word, is an inadequate term for what Isocrates did and taught. He himself never delivered speeches, though his numerous writings are mainly in the form of orations. Actually there was no traditional prose form in which a man could set forth his views and admonitions on politics or ethics. Imaginative poetry like epic and drama were of course impersonal, but even the monitory poems of Hesiod or Theognis are addressed to individuals, even epigrams on tombstones are couched in the form of a dialogue between the stone and the passer-by. The essays of Seneca or of Plutarch, to say nothing of St. Paul's, are in the form of epistles, or of orations which were never delivered, intended for an unidentified audience but addressed to a specific individual or group. How does one talk without at least an imagined interlocutor? A proper designation of Isocrates' own literary discourses is the political or ethical essay, and he is indeed a pioneer in the form.

It is the kind of knowledge which made Isocrates' own writings elegant and useful which he endeavored to teach to his pupils. Central in his program is *logos,* of which the simplest meaning is "word." *Logos* does not yet, of course, have the mystical meaning attached to it in the opening verse of the Fourth Gospel, "In the beginning was the word," but it is already on its way to becoming an independent entity almost with a will of its own. *Logos* means not only word, but discourse, story, a line of reasoning—anything that is "said." It is *logos* which distinguishes man from animals, and it is his greater abundance of *logoi* which distinguishes the superior man from the inferior. Man can think only in terms of *logos,* and the more *logoi* he possesses the more things he can think and the more subtle distinctions he can make. That is what makes Greeks superior to barbarians. Put in the form of a mathematical proposition, Greek is to barbarian as man is to animal. The use of "Greek" to signify "educated man" is common enough; what is important in Isocrates is that "Greek" means any educated man, even though he is racially a barbarian, if he shares the knowledge and outlooks of Greeks. In a memorable pasage (*Panegyricus* 50) Isocrates declares that Greek is defined not by race but by education. All of us, whatever our time and place, who have been shaped by Greek books are in this sense Greek.

A curriculum based on *logoi,* as Isocrates' was, is close to what we conceive of as a Liberal Arts program of study. Fundamental to the program is a library of classics which comprehend and present the cultural accumulations and traditions of the group. Explication of this body of literature involves, in the first place, a study of the artistic use of language, which might be emulated and refined in new works which the pupils might compose. This is the study of oratory in its narrower sense. If *logoi* are a mark of humanity, it is in keeping with the ideals of humanity to make them as artistic as possible.

But beyond questions of style, the study of literature must concern itself with ideas, with movements of history, careers of great personalities, standards of ethics, the ideals of the group which the literature summarizes, and the aspirations to which it points. In none of these particulars, perhaps, were Isocrates' graduates specialists—indeed Isocrates probably held, in opposition to Plato, that no man could be—but they were informed about the traditions of the race in the light of which new problems should be met, they could recognize what the new problems were, and they would seek a solution that might promote the general aspirations of the race.

Isocrates' alumni were numerous. Whereas the selected students of Plato's exclusive Academy were few in number and of limited influence, virtually all the notable orators and historians of the fourth century had been pupils of Isocrates. "From his school," as Cicero remarks, "as from the Horse of Troy none but leaders emerged." Aside from his refinements of style, which affected all subsequent artistic prose, the influence of Isocrates is perceptible in certain significant innovations in the writing of history. In the first place there was an effort to make history dramatic—those who disapproved called it sensational. By elaborating on pathetic scenes and on the psychological reactions of participants, and by manipulating materials in order to make changes of fortune manifest, a new and broader audience was attracted to history. It was the new type of history, in turn, which became the basis for the prose romance. Second, history became universal; whereas earlier historians (excluding Herodotus, who was the father of history) had concentrated attention upon Greece or upon part of it, now the whole world came into the historian's ken. Third, there was a new interest in the careers and personalities of the outstanding figures who shaped history. And, concomitantly, there was a tendency for history to be used for propagating favored political or ethical or patriotic attitudes. The approach, in terms of our context, was humanistic rather than scientific.

At the end of the fourth century B.C., the conquests of Alexander the Great revolutionized the Greek world. One consequence of the enormous widening of geographical and political horizons was a sudden diminution in the size of the individual, who was no longer sheltered within the

comfortable insulation of a city state. Reduced man had
to find some new attitude to preserve his self-sufficiency
in the overwhelmingly enlarged world. The happy few in
the Platonic tradition and the specialists in the Aris-
totelian had little help to offer. Both the new schools
which stepped in to redress the imbalance may be said
to derive in essential ways from the humanistic tradition.
Both Stoics and Epicureans addressed themselves not to
a privileged group but to the whole world, and both premised the basic equality of all men. Both were concerned
with spreading education. The Epicureans, indeed, took
the most significant step of all in making culture democratic: they introduced textbooks, even graded textbooks (the Greater Epitome and the Lesser), so that all
men might have access to learning, each according to his
capacity.

But to praise the humanism of Stoics and Epicureans
is not to minimize the solid achievements of Alexandrian
professionalism. Their work, in several departments, has
been of permanent value and the foundation upon which
later work was built; perhaps more important was their
charting of knowledge into various disciplines, each with
its rationale of scientific investigation. Whatever scholarly
work was done in Rome was naturally based upon Alexandrian models and Alexandrian spadework. But outside
laboratories and seminars, the Isocratean tradition survived in all parts of the Hellenistic world but most notably
in Rome, which was culturally the principal province of
that world. Everywhere, but especially in Rome, a strik-

ing consequence of specialization and technical advances in scholarship was to sharpen the distinction between professional and amateur.

To the Romans literary interests were never so vital as they had been to the Greeks; in time bookishness came to be considered a polite avocation for those who could afford the requisite leisure, but it was never an occupation weighty enough to pre-empt the time of serious Romans. The tough heroes of the Republic, as Cicero explains, were really as intelligent as they were high-minded but too much occupied with the vastly more important business of government and conquest to concern themselves with literature and philosophy. These things are desirable enough as gilding, but only after the solid monument has been built. Cicero's own great spurt of literary activity came, as he himself acknowledges, when he had been excluded from more important kinds of service to the state. His defense of the poet Archias, delivered when Cicero was at the height of his reputation and power, dwells upon the gentlemanly pleasures literature can afford, but the justification of poetry rests upon its usefulness to the state. The poet's work provides statesmen like Cicero with relaxation and with material for speeches, and it may serve as an incentive to high achievement by holding out a prospect of recording such achievement for posterity.

In Rome the difference between amateur and professional in letters as in other arts is decisive and unequivocal. The professional is a hireling, frequently and especially in philosophy a hireling Greek. That is why Roman writers on philosophy, Cicero no less than Seneca, insist that they are not professionals but amateurs. One thinks of the prophet Amos, who takes pains to announce that he is no prophet or prophet's son but a respectable keeper of sheep and of sycamore trees. Not in philosophy alone but in other pursuits which the Romans considered as mere appurtenances to civilized life, the same distinction obtained. Greek actors and athletes and artists suffered no diminution of status; Romans might idolize charioteers or gladiators but they disdained their work as servile. What offended Roman aristocrats most in Nero's freakish career was that he betrayed his class by acting, playing music, and engaging in athletic displays in person—in the Greek fashion. It has taken Europe a long while to shake off the Roman tradition of social disdain for performing artists and to return to the Greek view. First to recover not only respectability but even a superior status were the guild of bookmen.

V

BOOKISH EVANGELISM

THE distinguished Dutch medievalist and philosopher, Johan Huizinga, calls one of his most delightful and instructive books *Homo Ludens*. The point of the title is that the significant characteristic of the human species is not intellectuality, as the universally accepted *Homo Sapiens* implies, but playfulness, and Huizinga's subtitle is "A Study of the play element in culture." The pre-eminence of man over the rest of animal creation does indeed rest upon his intellectual capacities, but these are part of his natural endowment and are properly exercised in the spirit not of work but of play. Something of the notion Huizinga elaborates had been adumbrated, at least by implication, in the opening sentence of Aristotle's *Metaphysics,* which declares that "man by nature desires to know." Aristotle is not here admonishing his readers to pursue an intellectual life but, like a biologist, pointing out the most characteristic trait of a species: just as it is in the nature of a fish to swim or of a kitten to be playful, so it is in the nature of man to wish to know. If this curiosity is not fully operative, because it is not yet matured or is superannuated or is

41

dormant, man has not yet realized his proper character: that is why Aristotle says, in his *Ethics,* that a child or an old man or a man asleep is not capable of the happiness proper to man.

Huizinga suggests that all the significant advances made by humanity were made in a spirit of play. This is fairly obvious in the realms of fine arts, drama, and literature generally, but it is true in the sciences also. The initial insights upon which our astonishing and very welcome control of our physical world are based were conceived not by grim men busy in some technological laboratory but by impractical potterers with ideas in an essentially liberal arts atmosphere. In the past, at least, they have left their equations for the busy technologists to develop into marketable wares and have gone on with their own games. Even some happy technologists gleefully continue the games with I-beams and arches which absorbed them in childhood—and get paid for it.* Any impractical subject matter may be indirectly or incidentally useful.

Justification on the grounds of sheer playfulness applies more emphatically to the impractical subjects of humanistic education, and with greater emphasis in the degree that the subjects are more impractical. When I started my own teaching career, enrollments in Latin classes in the high schools were going into a spectacular decline, and in one school after another Latin was abandoned altogether. Teachers of the subject were naturally alarmed, and were desperately devising arguments to help stem the

---

* Dr. Johnson remarked that Greek was like lace, chiefly for show, not use; but when culture has passed the homespun stage an appetite for lace is not only legitimate but praiseworthy.

decline. I recall my first attendance at a meeting of classical teachers, where a set of arguments to be used with boards of education and similar authorities was being drawn up. The arguments all stressed the practical usefulness of studying Latin: it would enlarge vocabulary, improve spelling, enable students to surmise meanings of difficult words, and the like. I came near having my epaulettes stripped from my shoulders and my sword broken over the president's knee when I suggested that considerations of practicality were precisely the best arguments for abandoning Latin. In the first place, Latin did not necessarily do the things claimed for it; my own superb teacher of Latin was a wretched speller and his Latinate writing was virtually opaque. Then, even if Latin did improve spelling and vocabulary, the same ends could be achieved more directly and economically by using a good spelling book. The sole and sufficient reason for studying Latin, I then believed and still believe, is that it is fun to do so. People so constituted that it is incapable of affording them fun should not study Latin. It does indeed improve understanding and, sometimes, practice of the art and logic of language, it is a fine intellectual discipline, it does stretch the mind, and these things justify the time Latin takes when there are so many other things to learn. But the principal and essentially humanistic motivation must be fun—the kind of fun only the human species can enjoy. Other desirable consequences, however important they may be, are incidental.

In the Greek world, the most impressive example of the practical usefulness of what is, by definition, useless and undertaken for fun is, at the same time, the most spec-

tacular of all the practical achievements of the Greeks—
the Hellenization of the east after the conquests of Alexander the Great. Here is how Alexander's achievement is
described, some four hundred years after his time, in a
youthfully exuberant and rhetorical but essentially just
paragraph in Plutarch's *On the Fortune of Alexander:*

When Alexander civilized Asia Homer became
common reading, and the sons of Persians, Susia-
nians, and Gedrosians learned to intone the tragedies
of Sophocles and Euripides. And although Socrates
when tried on the charge of introducing foreign dei-
ties lost his cause to the informers who infested
Athens, yet through Alexander Bactria and the
Caucasus learned to revere the gods of the Greeks.
Plato wrote a book on the ideal state, but because
of its forbidding character he could not persuade
anyone to adopt it; but Alexander established more
than seventy cities among savage tribes, and sowed
all Asia with Grecian magistracies, and thus over-
came its uncivilized and brutish manner of living.
Although few of us read Plato's *Laws,* yet hundreds
of thousands have made use of Alexander's laws
and continue to use them. Those who were vanquished by Alexander are happier than those who es-
caped his hand; for these had no one to put an end
to the wretchedness of their existence, while the vic-
tor compelled those others to lead a happy life. . . .
Alexander's new subjects would not have been civilized had they not been vanquished; Egypt would
not have its Alexandria, nor Mesopotamia its

Seleuceia, nor Sogdiana its Prophthasia, nor India its
Bucephalia, nor the Caucasus the Greek City; for by
the founding of cities in these places savagery was
extinguished and the worse element, gaining familiarity with the better, changed under its influence. If,
then, philosophers take the greatest pride in civilizing
and rendering adaptable the intractable and untu-
tored elements in human character, and if Alexander
has been shown to have changed the savage natures
of countless tribes, it is with good reason that he
should be regarded as a very great philosopher.

A parallel to cultural transformation on so large a scale
that suggests itself to Americans is the spread of English
language and institutions in our continent. But Plutarch is
wrong in speaking of the natives whom Alexander civilized as savages. Whereas our sixteenth-century English
settlers found a sparse and primitive population not yet
emerged from the neolithic, the Greeks who followed
Alexander encountered populous and highly civilized nations with ancient traditions from whose ancestors the
ancestors of the Greeks had received much of their en-
lightenment. And yet in a short span the upper-class natives were speaking Greek and referring to themselves as
barbarians, adopting the dress and the usage of Greeks,
writing books in Greek or, when they wrote in their
vernaculars, following Greek literary forms and outlooks.

How was this accomplished? Not by force of arms:
Alexander's small expeditionary army and the Greek
forces of the Seleucid kings who followed him might

easily have been swallowed up in the larger mass of natives, with whom, indeed, as individuals they often merged.
The success of the conquest in the first instance was due
to superior techniques and livelier energies, and the success of the administration was due to superior organization; but what made the natives welcome the newcomers,
and what made it possible for the Greek element not only
to maintain its own character but to influence its environment, was Greek education.

The first thing any handful of Greeks did when they
formed a new settlement was to establish a school called
"gymnasium." The object of the gymnasium was to preserve the Greekhood of the group. The curriculum included calisthenics, of course, but it included literature
also. And the books that were studied were not, apparently, contemporary or recent works, but Homer and
tragedy which were, to all practical intents, as remote and
"classic" to the Hellenistic Greeks as they are to us. The
design is very clear. The objective was the same as
Isocrates', the same as that of our own Humanities courses
—to introduce young men to the tradition, the outlook,
and the aspirations of the group.

The administration of the Hellenistic gymnasium was
in the hands of the most eminent members of the community but, more important, "graduation" from the gymnasium was prerequisite to participation in the political
life of the community. The cities were managed, in effect,
by the alumni association of the gymnasium. It is easy to
see that upper-class natives would aspire to the privileges
which Greek education promised. The Greek language
and grounding in Hellenism were not only essential in

administration and in business but also for participation in cultural life and for social prestige.

What is of particular interest for the observer who likes to draw analogies with more modern attempts at cultural imperialism is that there was no organized program for cultural diffusion emanating from a central propaganda office in a capital. The Successor kings did indeed maintain the posture of alien conquerors rather than native dynasts, even after several generations, and they did continue to found "Greek" cities, or rather to change the name of an established native city and give it the constitution and institutions of a Greek *polis,* usually because the natives were willing to pay for the privilege. But the impulse to Hellenization was local and self-generated: natives saw that the Greek way was more enlightened and attractive and were eager to participate in it. Before very long Hellenized easterners were making their own contribution to the main stream of Greek culture, in literature, in philosophy, and even in the arts.

Virtually every site of any considerable Greek settlement in the Hellenized east, even far-off Babylon, contains the ruins of a Greek theater. Their seats are far too numerous to have been filled by immigrant Greeks and so must have been occupied by natives as well. People habituated to Greek drama and other cultural and political institutions of the Greeks would also wish to have public buildings and colonnades in the Greek style, and even if they retained their native religions they would erect temples in the Greek fashion, and even assimilate cult usages, in the matter of music and other appurtenances of worship, to Greek modes.

A not inconsiderable result of the wide diffusion of
Hellenism, then, was cultural homogeneity. Individual
countries and peoples in the Hellenistic *oikoumene* did
of course retain their native ethos as well as their native
vernaculars, at least in some levels of society, as is proven
by their re-emergence after the Greek force was spent;
but the common Greek factor in all was large enough so
that no educated citizen of one country would feel alien
in another. The physical aspects of the cities, their organization, and their cultural institutions were recognizably
similar. We know of one practical way in which cultural
homogeneity was recognized and encouraged: actors and
other "artists of Dionysus" belonged to an international
guild and might cross national boundaries freely even in
time of war. For those who look to the past for guidance
in the present, the function of a shared humanistic education in cementing disparate areas of a shrinking world
into a single *oikoumene* is peculiarly suggestive. Presently
we shall see that Erasmus in his turn sought to preserve
the totality of Europeanism against fragmentation by
making Latin a Pan-European medium of communication.

The new relationship between cultural survival and political survival has its own interest. All the world knew
that when a national sovereignty was extinguished, the religion which was inextricably bound up with it, and the
national culture which was bound up with religion, disappeared or was at least submerged. An international
culture, recognizably the same in such different nationalities as Egypt and Syria and Greece, was a new thing—

a thing larger than the nationalities within which it flourished, a thing, moreover, which could engage a deeper
commitment than the nationality in whose midst it had its
being. One effect of the teaching of Isocrates was to transform Hellenism itself into a kind of cult. The political
program which he never tired of advocating was a union
of the particularistic fragments of the Greek world under
some leader who would initiate a crusade against barbarian peoples in order to ensure the safety and the prosperity of the Hellenic ideal. The leaders he called upon
were such peripheral Hellenes as the kings of Macedonia
or Syracuse, and his views were naturally opposed by
such devoted patriots as Demosthenes, who would not
tolerate diminution of individual sovereignties in a Pan-
Hellenic organization. But the local view proved imprac-
tically romantic in the Hellenistic age; Isocrates' understanding of the situation was sounder. That Isocrates' concern was for Hellenic culture rather than merely Hellenic
domination is shown by his new definition of the title
"Greek." If Greek denotes a way of life rather than a
race, then the spread of Greek influence would concomitantly be a means for spreading the spiritual values of
Hellenism.

What insured the propagation and diffusion of Hellenism was the process of education. A way of life and
an outlook upon the world which is preserved and nur-
tured by a particular literature tend to take on the character of a cult, and it was the transformation of Hellenism
into a cult which enabled it to survive under the powerful
domination of Rome. The process had been going on,
consciously or otherwise, since the time of Isocrates; we

can see it most clearly in the career and works of Plutarch, in whose day Roman control of the Mediterranean was absolute and apparently destined to endure forever. Plutarch was born in Chaeronea in Boeotia, not far from Delphi, in the middle of the first century A.D. He himself studied in Athens, travelled, and must have been among the best educated men of his time. At an early age he was entrusted with important diplomatic missions. Like other gifted Greeks he settled in Rome, where he achieved professional and social success. And then, apparently at the height of his success, he deserted the world metropolis for his own provincial town, became market inspector of Chaeronea, priest of Delphi, and teacher to the young men of his neighborhood. The only explanation for this extraordinary conduct that Plutarch himself gives is in a delightful sentence at the opening of his *Life of Demosthenes:* it is a small town indeed that he lives in, but if he moved away it would be even smaller. But the nostalgia which motivated Plutarch, as we can see from his life and works, is more than an attachment to his native place.

It was rather a peculiar way of life that Plutarch wished to practice and promulgate, the way of life we call Hellenism, and his object was to make of Hellenism a cult whose values could not be affected by loss of political sovereignty. He attached himself to Delphi because insofar as Greek tradition possessed a focus, that focus was Delphi. He held whatever magistracy was available to him because active participation in public life was a part of Greek tradition. And most important, he discoursed to the youth of philosophy and literature and music and science, because concern in these matters was the sign manifest of Hellenism. The *Lives,* too, were written to inculcate loyalty to Hellenism. Their object was not, as has been thought, to introduce Greeks to Romans or Romans to Greeks, but to show Greeks that even their generals and statesmen had equalled or surpassed the Romans; there was no need to advertise Greek poets and philosophers and artists because in these categories the Romans themselves readily acknowledged Greek superiority. The totality of the past, for Plutarch, provides not only the truest example but the highest sanction for civilized and humane conduct in the present, and it was the duty of those who had a special loyalty to Hellenism to spread its values abroad among peoples whose own past was not so privileged but who were yet susceptible to the evangel. The operative factor is education—the kind of education we call humanistic.

Plutarch's response to the challenge of lost or diminished sovereignty is education, and education would appear to be the only device capable of ensuring cultural survival regardless of political vicissitudes. It was precisely the same response which ensured cultural survival under Roman domination for another literate people strongly attached to a way of life crystallized in a literature. When Jerusalem was under siege by Vespasian and Titus in A.D. 70, friend and foe alike believed that the fall of the city would mean the extinction of its peculiar culture. Before the city fell, we are told, Johanan ben Zakkai (who was roughly contemporary with Plutarch) had himself spirited out of it in a symbolical coffin, and proceeded to Jamnia where he collected a band of students who devoted themselves to the study of the literature which contained the premises, outlooks, and aspirations they cherished. The compelling motive for resistance to any diminution of political sovereignty is concern for peculiar national cultural values. Plutarch and Johanan show how these values can not only be preserved but transmitted to posterity, if commitment to them is strong enough. The means to this end is education: its efficacy is amply attested by the important ingredients in our own culture which derived from Athens and Jerusalem after both had lost political sovereignty.

The most powerful of all witnesses to the proposition that a way of life, which can claim deep commitment, can survive and flourish through education, regardless of its political status, is Christianity, which included elements drawn from both Hellenism and Judaism. The most spectacular and the most momentous achievement of Hellenistic education is that it endowed nascent Christianity with the outward forms which alone enabled it to assert itself as a world religion. It could hardly have become so in the hands of the humble Palestinians, innocent of the larger world, who first undertook to propagate it. It was at Antioch, which was a major center of Hellenistic education and a seething microcosm of Hellenistic fusion, and by the agency of men educated in Greek that the word Christian was first used, that Christianity became Greek-speaking, that it received the outward form and the philosophical framework which made it accessible and welcome to the entire civilized world. It was at Antioch that the doctrines and organization of the Church were crystallized and that Christianity first encountered and achieved a *modus vivendi* in the gentile world, in Antioch

that the Fourth Gospel was probably written, that
Theophilus made the New Testament into scripture, that
Lucian established the text of it which we still use, that
the Council of Nicaea was planned, that Arius learned
his doctrine, that John Chrysostom and other great fourth-
century doctors received their superb secular, as well
as theological, training. It was through the substance
and techniques of the Hellenistic educational system as
practised in Antioch, in a word, that Christianity not only
adopted Greek modes of expression but very soon reached
a social and intellectual level which assured it respectable
standing outside its own communion. From Antioch it
could proceed westward not as an obscure cult of the ignorant and underprivileged but as a movement of established respectability.

From many points of view the Hellenistic age is one of
the most instructive, as well as most seminal, in the history of European civilization. And the chief moral of the
story, at least in our present context, is that the closest
tie that binds men together is a shared experience of a
common literary tradition. Men who eat the same kinds
of food or wear the same styles of clothing or live in the
same kinds of climate understand one another better than
men who do not. But those who understand one another
most fully are those who have read the same books.

The humanistic tradition which originated in Greece
spread eastward when geographical horizons were enlarged and then west to Rome and thence north to Europe. What homogeneity Europe and its transmarine ap-

panages possess is due to the cultural cement. But what of the farther east? To the Hellenistic Greeks the word *oikoumene* meant the inhabited world—so far as they knew it, but now the world has shrunk, and it is becoming increasingly necessary for portions heretofore insulated to understand one another. To this end the first practical step is to learn the cultural traditions of the east in somewhat the same fashion as we learn our own. For learning and teaching our own cultural legacy an effective device is the Humanities program I have spoken of, and a similar program might serve as an economical introduction to the cultures of the East. In 1948-1949 an experimental course of this character was introduced into my own college, with myself as one of the experimenters. The reading was in works of Chinese, Japanese, and Indian literature which were suitable and available in translation. The course was so far successful that it has become a regular part of the undergraduate program. The reading list has been enlarged and improved, and translations of specific central and seminal works have been made for the use of students in the course. When the course was initiated, precisely the same kind of objections were adduced by specialists as had been adduced when the original Humanities course was initiated: these remote and difficult works were a preserve for philologers and should not be tampered with by laymen. But, as in the case of the older course, serious students who had participated in it sometimes attained a more meaningful understanding of their materials than some specialists possess. The greatest advantage education can offer is that it enables a short-lived and time-bound individual to move in several cultural climates simultaneously, and even a fragmentary acquaintance with a culture hitherto obscure is a worth-while increment. But the remoter advantage of increasing mutual understanding to the end of promoting the unity of mankind is surely a consideration.

VI

SAINTS AND FOOLS

Each June on a thousand college campuses, a thousand college presidents swathed in robes which mark them as current masters of an ancient mystery, bestow diplomas upon young men swathed in robes which show that they have become approved journeymen in the mystery, and pronounce some such formula as this: "By the authority vested in me I confer upon you the degree of X with all the privileges and immunities thereunto appertaining." By whom the authority has been vested is usually left somewhat vague; it may be the state legislature, or a board of trustees, or the time-honored usages of the guild of scholars, or, more probably, a combination of all of these. "The privileges and immunities thereunto appertaining" are even more vague. A cynic might remark that the only privilege conferred by a liberal arts diploma was that of paying dues to an alumni association, and the only immunity freedom from ever having to read another book. There are of course tangible advantages in possessing a liberal arts college diploma, especially one adorned with ivy, for membership committees in many clubs and personnel officers in many corporations are interested in such matters, and we are told that college graduates earn x thousands of dollars more during their working lives than unfortunates without college degrees. But these can scarcely be the privileges and immunities intended in the solemn presidential formula.

When I try to find a concrete meaning for the formula (always a dangerous proceeding in the language of ritual) the best I can think of is that it makes the person to whom it is uttered a member of an elect—which is itself enough to bring blushes in a democratic society. But the simple fact is that until yesterday or the day before a humanistic education *was* the key for admission to an elect, and at certain periods the term elect even carried its theological connotations: scholarship was actually believed to insure a man a favored position in the world to come. It is of some interest to see how this belief arose, most markedly in the last pre-Christian century, and how vestiges of it persisted until the nineteenth century.

In ancient Greece, as in certain other societies, the educational program moved between two poles which have been termed knightly and scribal. The knightly ideal is the one premised in Homer: what Phoenix taught Achilles were the accomplishments and conduct appropriate for a gentleman, and the first four books of the *Odyssey* are what the Germans call a *Bildungsroman,* showing, in effect, how Telemachus was educated to take his place as a responsible squire. The education of the gentleman amateur of which I have spoken above is a continuation of the knightly ideal, though the aristocratic society out of which that ideal grew had given way to democratic institutions. The notion of a gentleman's education persisted, with vicissitudes, through the ages. It is clearly present in Rome, where gentlemen scholarly enough to write philosophic treatises, like Cicero or Seneca, felt constrained to protest that they were not professionals but amateurs. It is clearly the principle which informed education in eighteenth-century England.

Where the books which constitute the curriculum claim supernatural inspiration, as many early works did, or when even secular books came to be looked upon as a kind of scripture, as happened in later antiquity, the expertise of the scholar who studies and teaches them tends to take on something of a sacerdotal character. Wherever learning is valued the scholar is respected and even loved. But where extraordinary powers are attributed to him, the popular attitude of affectionate respect shifts to one of awed reverence. Where religious leadership does not depend upon a chain of transmission of charismatic authority, the only license which sets the leader above lay communicants is expertise in a particular literature. The principal function of such a leader is in fact teaching, but the quasi-sacerdotal character of his office gives him the power to confer upon his pupils something more than ability to pass an examination. For this type of scholarship and education an appropriate term is scribal.

The antecedents for the scribal type of education in Greece are as ancient as those for the knightly. An easy index for the whole complex of ideas is whether or not inspiration is claimed for poetic utterances: the man who explains what the prophet has said is often a priest. Plato believed that men who expound inspired poetry share to some degree in the inspiration of their subject matter. To say nothing of the remote Orpheus, who may or may not have been historical, Pythagoras and Empedocles plainly claimed supernatural inspiration for their utterances. Homer, who often seems to be in conscious opposition to the Orphic strand of belief, does indeed invoke the Muses, especially where the faculty of memory is needed, but he claims no special prerogatives for himself. But Hesiod and Pindar do claim to be the special wards of the Muses, and it is clear that they meant this claim to be taken literally. Plato's belief in poetic inspiration is expressed in a number of passages; in the *Phaedrus,* for example, he says: "Whoever knocks at the door of poetry without the Muses' frenzy, persuaded that by art alone he will be a sufficient poet, fails of perfection, and the work of the sober is forthwith eclipsed by that of the frenzied."

Often, of course, and especially in later poets, the claim to inspiration and divine favor is no more than a literary cliché. When Roman Horace, who professes to be a minister of the Muses, declares *non omnis moriar,* "I shall not wholly die," it is merely an assertion of the artist's pride; he will not die because the monument he has builded is more enduring than bronze. But we cannot always be so sure. A poem of Sappho addressed to "a woman of no education" reads: "When you are dead you will lie unremembered for evermore; for you have no part in the roses that come from Pieria; nay, obscure here, you will move obscure in the house of Death, and flit to

and fro among such of the dead as have no fame." It may
be that Sappho, too, is merely asserting the artist's pride,
and that the immortality she implies for herself is, like
Horace's, an immortality of reputation. But the lines do
not give the impression of hyperbole. There is a strong
likelihood that Sappho had a special connection with
Orphism, and this may be the basis of her assurance of
immortality. At any rate, we can see the origin of the
curious epithet *doctus* or *docta* ("learned") applied to a
poet as high praise; and we can also see that the poet's
claim to immortality has a long history, however thinned
down the conception of his immortality may have become.

In the classical period, so far as our literary evidence goes,
the knightly type of education prevailed over the scribal, as
the rational approach of Isocrates prevailed over the mystical approach of Plato. But it was Isocrates himself who
propagated the notion that the classical literature was the
repository of cherished Hellenism. Partly because of the
new status of literature as a kind of scripture, but partly also
surely, under the influence of the eastern modes of education which the Greeks then encountered, Greek education
in the Hellenistic age tended towards the scribal program.
The principal object of eastern education was to perpetuate
a guild of professional scribes. In Egypt, where different
types of writing and, in Mesopotamia, where different languages were used simultaneously, great technical proficiency was demanded of the scribe and his services were
indispensable. He functioned not only in the bureaucracy,
but part of his duty was the guardianship of specialized
tradition, including codes of prudential wisdom. In Israel

the scribal stage came much later than in other countries of the east, but it was the prevailing form after Ezra,
who is himself called a scribe. In the Greek and "barbarian" worlds alike, the man recognized as scribe enjoyed
a special status and, where immortality was reckoned with,
special advantages in the world to come.

"Of all our qualities," says Plutarch in his *On Educating
Children,* "learning alone is immortal and divine." Stal-
wart Hellene as Plutarch was, he was also a convinced
Platonist; his statement cannot be dismissed as hyperbole,
for it appears that education came actually to be regarded
as a guarantee of immortality. A remarkable number of
inscriptions and tomb decorations of Plutarch's and the
preceding century represent the deceased as a *mousikos
aner,* a protégé of the Muses or, in our own language, the
holder of a baccalaureate degree in humanistic studies. Recording the fact on his tombstone amounted to an explicit
claim that the man so qualified would profit in the world
to come. In the *Axiochus,* included in the Platonic corpus
but actually a work of the first century B.C., the chief delights of the Elysian Fields are represented as "discussions
for the philosophers, theaters for the poets, dancing, con-
certs, intelligent conversation round the banquet table."
Those capable of such rare delights, it was believed, would
be vouchsafed them. Education is endowed with a mystic quality which makes of it an object of religion.

From time to time during the centuries which followed,
a priestly kind of dignity was claimed by scholars or
thrust upon them, even when the promise of immortality
was reduced to a promise of enduring reputation. Some
remarks on the esteem in which scholarship was held, by

scholars and by others, will come more appropriately in later pages; here two or three examples will be enough to indicate how far extravagant respect for scholarship persisted. In the Humanist age, Erasmus, in his quality as scholar, not as thinker or artist, enjoyed an esteem not surpassed in extent and intensity by any general or artist or writer or actor or athlete in modern times. On the other hand, the self-esteem of the University Wits who scorned their less privileged Elizabethan rivals, is as ludicrous as it was arrogant. At the beginning of our own century Theodor Mommsen received the Nobel prize in literature not because he was a great writer but because he was a distinguished scholar in Roman history. Perhaps the most startling evidence for the prestige to which a man who knew Greek felt himself entitled, even including emoluments in the world to come, is the bland declaration of Thomas Gaisford (1779–1855) who was himself, naturally, a Greek scholar: "The advantages of a classical education are twofold—it enables us to look down with contempt on those who have not shared its advantages, and also fits us for places of emolument, not only in this world, but in that which is to come."

That these remarks are not the vaporing of an insulated and naive scholar is proven by the fact that knowledge of Greek has for so long been a prerequisite for appointments in the Foreign Office, and in other branches of the British public service. Apparently the grating was effective, for the services which set it up have been notably skilful. The grating was used with more obvious propriety during the war, when it became necessary to train numbers of men quickly in the use of the Japanese language.

In the United States selection was made on the basis of membership in Phi Beta Kappa, and the results were satisfactory. In England, which has no equivalent to our Phi Beta Kappa, selection was made on the basis of high achievement in Greek, on the reasonable theory that a man able to learn one difficult language could learn another, and the results were satisfactory also. By analogous reasoning, doubtless, men clever and persistent enough to learn Greek will probably prove to be clever and patient diplomats and administrators. But one case, which I myself encountered during the past year, gives me pause. A native of a newly liberated African state applied for admission to candidacy for a higher degree in my department. When I asked him whether he was strongly attracted to the study of Greek and whether he wished to teach it, he told me frankly that neither was the case; what he aspired to was a high position in the government of his country, and he was convinced, from what he knew of British practice, that a degree in Greek would open all doors to him.

There were men who deflated the exaggerated claims, first for the teachings of the poets and then for the teachings of the scholars, almost as soon as they were made. The pre-Socratics criticized Homer and even Hesiod on moral grounds. Xenophanes complained that "Homer and Hesiod assigned to the gods all that is disgraceful and blameworthy among men—stealing and adultery and mutual deceit." When Pythagoras visited Hades he saw Homer and Hesiod enduring the punishments of the damned for what they had said about the gods; and Heraclitus used to say that "Homer deserved to be chased out

of the lists and beaten with rods." The most notorious
denigrator of Homer in the late classical period was
Zoilus, whose virulence earned him the epithet *Homero-
mastix,* or Scourge of Homer. Zoilus was a Cynic, and his
motive, like that of his spiritual descendant Pococurante
in *Candide,* was to flaunt his scorn of conventional views.

Criticism of the pretensions of teachers and of the aberrations of scholarship are more damaging because they are
frequently better founded. The earliest and funniest of all
is Aristophanes' in the *Clouds.* Here the teaching of gen-
ders in grammar is made as absurd as the study of the
habits of gnats and fleas. But Aristophanes' genre is comedy, and here, at least, his satire is without rancor. Lucian,
who followed him by half a millennium, is generally concerned only with amusing his auditors, but his persistent
deflation of self-seeking and dishonest teachers is seriously
intended; he has no criticism of honest teachers. Lucian
indulges in an occasional hit at scholars also. In his *True
History,* for example, he takes advantage of an encounter
with Homer in the Elysian Fields to ask the interpretation
of a line about which scholars had disputed: had he in
fact meant what was attributed to him? "I don't know,"
the puzzled Homer replied, "it popped into my head that
way."

Concern with trivial minutiae and excessive ingenuity
have always been more or less justifiable charges against
philological scholarship, and these, too, begin in antiquity.
Here is what Seneca, who disdained professionalism, has
to say: "It is no more to the point for me to investigate
whether Homer or Hesiod was the older poet than to know
why Hecuba, although younger than Helen, showed her

years so lamentably. What would be the point in trying to determine the respective ages of Achilles and Patroclus? Do you raise the question, 'Through what regions did Ulysses stray?' instead of trying to prevent ourselves from going astray at all times? We have no leisure to hear lectures on the question whether he was sea-tost between Italy and Sicily or outside our known world." And this is how Tiberius, who was a Philistine, teased the grammarians: "Tiberius used to test even the grammarians, a class of men in whom he was especially interested, by questions something like this: 'Who was Hecuba's mother?' 'What was the name of Achilles among the maidens?' 'What were the Sirens in the habit of singing?' "

The pedantry, which is the inevitable accompaniment of good philology, naturally made its appearance in the Humanist revival also. Montaigne, whose great master was Seneca, has a sharp essay, *On Pedantry,* in which he speaks scornfully of men who are "grammarians, not gentlemen." The actual words of Seneca are echoed more closely in John Webster's *The Duchess of Malfi.* This is how Bosola, who is as clever as he is unprincipled, is described: "I knew him in Padua—a fantastical scholar, like such who study to know how many knots was in Hercules' club, of what colour Achilles' beard was, or whether Hector were not troubled with the toothache. He hath studied himself half blear-ey'd to know the true symmetry of Caesar's nose by a shoeing-horn; and this he did to gain the name of a speculative man."

Ridicule like this has been the lot of philological scholarship up to the present day, and at some points, as we shall presently see, it has been so shrewdly aimed as to

make philologers squirm. But humanistic scholarship and
teaching, carried on in the spirit of Seneca and Montaigne,
is immune. In any discipline it is easy for a wag to ridicule the bricks out of which the larger structure must be
built. There may be some point, for example, in the description of laboratory psychologists as latter-day magi-
cians who pull habits out of rats, but no one seriously
questions the value of psychology, and no one need seriously question the value of the study of the classics because
some of its professors have claimed to be saints and others
have been condemned as fools. In a beautiful poem called
"Gathering Leaves," Robert Frost says a word in behalf
of insubstantial kinds of crops. Of his harvest of leaves he
says:

> *Next to nothing for weight,*
> *And since they grew duller*
> *From contact with earth,*
> *Next to nothing for color.*
>
> *Next to nothing for use.*
> *But a crop is a crop,*
> *And who's to say where*
> *The harvest shall stop?*

VII
HUMANIST REVIVAL

AT SEVERAL conjunctures in history there have been marked upsurges of interest in classical literature as an object of study and emulation. In the second century A.D., for example, in the movement which has been called the Second Sophistic, litterateurs scorned their immediate antecedents and adopted the modes of the ancients as the only proper models for writing and teaching. The hollowness of their efforts demonstrates the futility of any archaizing movement. At the end of the eighteenth and beginning of the nineteenth century, under the stimulus of men like Winckelmann and Schlegel, there was enthusiastic admiration not so much for the form and content as for what were believed, often mistakenly, to be the aesthetic ideals of the classics. Our generation is experiencing a lesser resurgence, but this is based rather on the poetic techniques and on views of man and the world characteristic of the classical authors. In both these particulars the practices and views of our own literature and criticism are in fact closer to the Greek than those of any intervening age have been. But the greatest and most mo-

mentous of all the upsurges is of course the one called
the revival of learning, or the Renaissance.

None of the upsurges, not even that of the Renaissance,
can properly be called a revival, for the classics were continuously present and continuously operative. Even during
the Middle Ages, even in the tenth which was the darkest
of all the centuries, study and emulation of some classical
authors went on. The Renaissance comes closest to being
a literal revival because so many books which had fallen
into oblivion were discovered anew, because so many
more people became interested in classical books, because
they were studied with greater sophistication and without
the limitations and constraints of the earlier period, and,
most important for the history of ideas and educational
ideals, because the forms and ideas found in the ancient
books materially altered contemporary modes of expression and contemporary conceptions of man and the world.
Each of the more significant humanist writers seems to
take up an important conversation just where the ancient
interlocutors left off.

But the humanists, unlike their predecessors, were aware
that there was a millennium of interruption in the con-
versations. Their approach, like ours, was essentially antiquarian; the phenomena under study ran their course
and reached their consummation in the past, and could
be scrutinized and evaluated objectively. Of Dante we can
sense that he felt himself a continuator of the spirit of
Vergil which had descended to him in an unbroken line,
as in a sense he was. But Machiavelli, who knew more of
the ancients and whose greater sophistication enabled him
to find more kinds of things in them, looked at their ex-

perience and wisdom across a wide gulf, as we do. He could exploit their work for permanent principles and relevant analogies to apply to the contemporary scene, as he does with acute insight in his *Discourses on the First Decade of Titus Livy,* but this is not the same thing as a patriot dealing with an earlier stretch of the history of his people.

The initial stages of the revival, which involved the discovery and publication of forgotten texts (but they did exist, and some had been well used!) and zealous study of Greek, bear the characteristics of what I have spoken of as the scribal type of study and teaching. Men like Petrarch, Boccaccio, and especially Poggio searched out unfamiliar texts, and Greek teachers like Chrysoloras, Gemistos Plethon, and Bessarion found eager pupils in Italy. It is worth noting of Petrarch and Boccaccio that the pedantic works on which they prided themselves (including Petrarch's Latin epic called *Africa*) are forgotten, while the authors are remembered for vernacular works they themselves thought frivolous. Petrarch's fanatical devotion to Cicero gave rise to a cult of Ciceronianism which refused to tolerate any word or usage not found in the pages of Cicero. The Church objected that it was unchristian to imitate the pagans, but by the sixteenth century, under the leadership of Cardinal Bembo, a society of literati bound its members by oath not to use any word which could not be found in the pages of Cicero. Though he was a prelate and papal secretary to Leo X, Bembo could not mention the Holy Ghost and speaks of the Virgin Mary as *dea ipsa.* The Church is *respublica,* its officials *magistri,* saints are *divi,* cardinals *senatores,* nuns are *virgines vestales,* and dating is by Kalends, Nones, and Ides. Scribal classicism so rigid would of course make Latin a dead language; being incapable of expressing new things and new ideas, it must remain an esoteric medium for a scribal clique. Men who had outgrown the initial pedantry of the revival and who, like Pico della Mirandola and others, were more concerned for the liberating ideas of burgeoning humanism, objected to the Procrustean strait jacket, and there were heated polemics on the subject. The logical answer to the Ciceronians on their own philological grounds was that if the pages of our extant Cicero, which contain words Cicero uses only once, had been worm-eaten or damp-stained, we should be deprived of even those words. A more compelling answer on humanistic grounds is implicit in the work of Erasmus.

Of Erasmus' enormous reputation, bestowed upon him in his quality as "scribe," I have spoken above. The strange thing is that by modern standards he was not a good scribe. His contemporaries esteemed him for his numerous well-printed editions of ancient books, which included the New Testament and several of the Fathers of the Church. But though his knowledge was broad and exact Erasmus was not in fact a good editor, for he was capable of preferring an inferior manuscript which was handsomely written to a superior but ill-written one. Of greater importance, in retrospect, was his effort to make Latin viable by accommodating it to contemporary needs.

The significance of this design is impossible to exaggerate. It is of a different quality than the contrivance of a code for communication among initiates in a charmed circle, of a different quality than the revival of Gaelic in

Eire or of Hebrew in Israel. Its objective was not to set one group apart from the main stream of Europeanism but rather to preserve Europeanism against the danger of fragmentation. Since Erasmus' day individuals, concerned to promote mutual understanding among the peoples of Europe, have invented "international" languages, all of which must fail simply because they *are* invented. But Latin had been, and might have continued to be, a cement for Europeanism. And the culture for which Latin was to be the medium was not to be restricted to one people or class. What Erasmus objected to most in his world was war and superstition and ignorance. His concern for Europeanism explains why Erasmus did not support Luther though he was at first attracted to his reforms: Luther's success would be a disruptive force in the unity of Europe, and the Church Catholic, whatever its shortcomings, was a force for cohesion. Doubtless the forces which contribute to nationalism would have divided Europe in any case; we can at least be wistful over Erasmus' failure, and admire him for his effort.

His principles for the use and teaching of Latin, Erasmus laid down in his *Ciceronianus,* and he illustrated the adequacy of Latin to the needs of daily life, at every level, in his *Colloquies.* Of all Erasmus' works the *Colloquies* are today the most attractive to the largest number of readers. Some find them models of the short story or genre sketch, and some delight in their satire of superstitions connected with religious pilgrimages, the ignorance of the lower clergy, the greed of mendicant friars, whether for doctrinal reasons or simply because they are graceful and witty and amusing. The *Colloquies* are indeed good stories and good satire, but they are designed to be a phrase-book, such as one might use for learning the idioms of any foreign language, and the art and satire are incidental.

The book starts with forms of greeting, how one should address a young man or an old, an old man of superior station ("father") or inferior ("uncle"), what one says to a person entering a hospital or recovered from an illness, and the like. The phrases grow into paragraphs and the paragraphs into sketches as the student advances and the teacher wishes to provide him with richer material. Students with restless minds frequently find themselves on the way to such sketches in a dragging classroom. "The gloves of my aunt are on the conservatory table," says the book. "Why was my aunt so flustered she left her gloves?" wonders the student. "Who else was in the conservatory? And where was my uncle all this while?" Ancient rhetoricians who trained lawyers concocted cases involving pirates and lovers, and these have been thought to be the origins of the plots in the late Greek romances, to have left their precipitate in the *Gesta Romanorum,* and thus eventually, through Boccaccio and Chaucer, to have helped shape the European genre of the short story. The longest of Erasmus' *Colloquies,* called in translations "The Religious Treat" or "The Godly Feast," brings in, naturally and unobtrusively, a rich conversation involving plants and animals, food and dress, books and ideas, and is withal a diverting sketch.

In his own day the most widely circulated of Erasmus' works was his *Adagia,* which is a collection, enlarged from edition to edition, of quotable nuggets from ancient authors. Today such a work would be compiled by a hack, euphemistically called a researcher, who would quarry his material from earlier collections going back to Erasmus, and it would be used for adorning ornate prose with purple passages. But in its own day Erasmus' *Adagia* could properly be described as an educational work and was used as such. It skimmed the cream (or what contemporaries regarded as the cream) of all classical literature and provided a wide public with a conspectus, however partial, of classical thought. At the same time it afforded a chrestomathy of the Latin language at its lapidary best.

Whatever we may think of Erasmus' larger design to make Latin a practical means of communication for every need, his *Colloquies* and *Adagia* show him to be a master teacher. His pupils learn the refinements of language, but at the same time their minds are stretched in other directions also, and receive their initiation into the humanistic legacy. Modern teachers of Latin who grow footsore with marching with Caesar may well turn to the *Colloquies* for relief; I myself have sometimes done so, to the great satisfaction of my students. That Erasmus' intentions were in fact humanistic is made plain by the misgivings at preoccupation with classical literature expressed by men like Thomas à Kempis.

The name of Erasmus suggests that of his friend Thomas More, who was deeply involved in high politics and a significant and systematic political theorist, but who, like all the humanists, was much concerned with education. So far as posterity is concerned More's great achievement is the *Utopia,* whose immediate design, as is clear from the introductory book, is to prevent the exploitation of the weak by the strong by means of abolishing the institution of private property. It is to this end that equality in dress, housing, food, and other externals is enforced upon the Utopians. The regimen is reminiscent of that in Plato's *Republic,* which was More's model; but whereas Plato's self-sufficient and disciplined state seems to be an end in itself, Utopia is not. The efficiency of the economy and the elimination of conspicuous consumption are calculated to allow the greatest possible quantity of leisure to the individual, and the discipline is a police measure to insure that the leisure, which is the objective of the whole system, is to be used for education. It is not expected that everyone will rise for the early morning lectures or engage in the after-dinner discussions; every man will participate in intellectual exercises in proportion to his interests and abilities, but every man is encouraged to develop his intellectual capacities to the full limit of his abilities.

Precisely what the educational programs consisted of is not specified, but there are hints. In the past the Utopians had chanced to receive a large parcel of Greek manuscripts, some damaged by ship rats and otherwise; the Utopians had managed to learn the language and had studied the books to good effect. Presumably these books and the ideas derived from them were the basis of Utopian education. Clearly they had not only mastered the language but had learned certain of the outlooks which European humanists had also learned. What is noticeable to the reader who approaches More by way of his European antecedents is a rational approach to religion and a purposeful deflation of the romantic glorification of war and of love.

In Utopia everyone believed in God, but no particular

form of belief or observance was mandatory. It was forbidden for the proponent of one form of belief to denigrate another, and it was forbidden to preach hell-fire too ardently. Tolerance is often a euphemism for indifference; in More's case it was definitely not, for he suffered martyrdom for his faith when it was very easy to recant. He did indeed persecute heretics, but here his motive was much like Erasmus': he did not wish to see European unity disrupted. More's prescriptions for war are at least as startling. War, being an ugly and inhuman thing, is to be waged through vulgar foreign mercenaries and through a system of bounties for the assassination (or voluntary defection) of enemy leaders and officers. Indeed the state's only reason for accumulating gold (which was discredited for ordinary use by being limited to prisoners' chains and chamber pots) was to save Utopians from soiling their hands and their spirits by war. Nothing could be more antithetic to the ideal of chivalry. And nothing could be more antithetic to romance than the Utopian system of arranging marriages. No one would buy even a horse, reason the Utopians, without asking the dealer to remove its saddle; accordingly, before a marriage is entered into in Utopia, the bride and groom must be exhibited to each other unclothed—of course under the chaperonage of sober elders. More himself, then, is also a master teacher; in his view, indeed, education is mankind's single most important enterprise.

There were, of course, many other humanists, many of whom were teachers in the literal sense and wrote textbooks for their students or books about teaching. Associated with Erasmus and More was an English group

which included John Colet, William Grocyn and Thomas
Linacre. Thomas Elyot made the first Latin-English dic-
tionary and wrote a sensible treatise on education called
The Book Named the Governor. Best known of all as
teacher and theorist was Roger Ascham, who taught Queen
Elizabeth her Greek and was also a diplomat. Ascham's
great work is the *Scholemaster*. Unlike Erasmus who was
so far a citizen of Europe that he would resent being
called a Dutchman, these men were all Englishmen, concerned to give other Englishmen a liberal education. From
their day almost until ours, the classics remained the
mainstay of English education because, in John Milton's
phrase, they enriched the mind, sharpened the intellect,
and purified taste.

One other Latin-writing humanist I wish to mention
because of a special attachment is the Scot, George
Buchanan; for a year in a far country, his collected poetical
works minutely printed in a tiny volume, was the only
book I had to read, and I read it all and still love the
writer. The general reader is apt to remember Buchanan
only from Montaigne's mention of him as his teacher at
Bordeaux. There he gave his pupils Latin plays to act—
the *Alcestis* and *Medea* which he translated from Euripides (the choice shows that he understood these plays
as attacks on the disabilities imposed on women), and
Jephthah's Daughter and *John the Baptist* which he wrote
himself. Both are liberal in outlook; *John the Baptist,* in
particular, is a ringing attack on autocratic rule. When he
was imprisoned by the Inquisition in Portugal, Buchanan
translated the Psalms into lyric meters, chiefly Horatian;
what is of interest here is not only the excellence of the
translation but Buchanan's realization of the fact that the

Psalms are in fact fine lyric poems and might be enjoyed as such. Buchanan's longest work is a six-book hexameter poem called *Sphaera,* which attempts to defend the geocentric theory of the universe against the newly proposed heliocentric theory. Buchanan was mistaken, but the *Sphaera* shows the wide scope of humanist curiosity and the sense of wonder generated by new knowledge. Why have not such sweeping phenomena as the nebular hypothesis or atomic fission generated poetry?

More interesting, in our context, is the satirical *Franciscanus,* which is the longest of Buchanan's numerous minor poems. Here, among other things, Buchanan describes the school in Paris where he taught—the arrogant and irascible teacher who beat his pupils, the sniveling and puzzled boys whose minds were left untouched. One senses Buchanan's shock at the iniquity of so abusing texts like Vergil, and at the greater iniquity of so abusing pupils who would profit by real teaching. It is pleasant to record that Buchanan ended his life as the first and highly respected principal of Aberdeen University.

It is inevitable, when the visionary afflatus calcifies into scribalism, that pedantry like the Parisian teacher's should assert itself and should sometimes come near to choking the humanistic tradition with unimaginative dullness; but the visionaries have their own progeny. Here is a picture of the pedant as drawn in Yeats' "The Scholars":

> *Bald heads forgetful of their sins,*
> *Old, learned, respectable bald heads*
> *Edit and annotate the lines*
> *That young men, tossing on their beds,*

Rhymed out in love's despair
To flatten beauty's ignorant ear.

All shuffle there; all cough in ink;
All wear the carpet with their shoes;
All think what other people think;
All know the man their neighbour knows.
Lord, what would they say
Did their Catullus walk that way?

The point is that there is usually a Yeats to restore perspective.

For all their merits and even their occasional contemporary timeliness, the principal interest of the humanistic Latin writings is as monuments in cultural history. Their authors gathered up and sometimes distilled the fruits of the revival, and they provided both materials and a climate for writers in the vernaculars. Without such preparation the vernacular authors could not have written as they did, and could not have found appreciative audiences if they had. But without the vernacular authors, since Europe was after all not all Latin-speaking, the humanistic impulse must surely have dried up. But the transition was gradual. The earliest significant writers in the vernacular languages were themselves steeped in the Latin authors, and it is plain that they expected their first audiences to have some knowledge of Latin. Rabelais who of all authors seems the most vulgar (in all the meanings attached to that word) is learned as well as intelligent, and expects learning as well as intelligence of his readers. Montaigne's

Essays or Burton's *Anatomy of Melancholy* are peppered
with untranslated quotations from the ancients, and if, as
is not unlikely, these were quarried out of Erasmus' collection called *Adagia,* the readers of Montaigne and Burton could probably be counted on to know the *Adagia,*
which was possibly the most widely circulated book of its
time.

Questions of educational practice and theory are at least
as prominent in the vernacular writers as in the Latin.
There are particularly notable passages in both Rabelais
and Montaigne, who are doubtless the most widely known
and admired of the continental humanists, and a word
must be said about each. The specific program of the new
education, its procedures and its theory, is set forth in
detail in Rabelais and given added emphasis by a contrast
with the stultifying program which it replaced. Chapters
21 and 22 of Rabelais' first book describe Gargantua's
education at "that lousy college," the Sorbonne, which was
calculated to make him not only ignorant but also beastly.
All that he learned was to mumble sundry prayers by rote
without the least comprehension of their meaning, all that
he heard were endless mumbled masses and homilies. He
was encouraged in laziness, gluttony, and uncleanly personal habits. His exercise consisted of rolling and stretch-
ing in bed, his games were only such as could be played
sitting down. Nothing was ever done to awaken intellect
or prick curiosity.

The improved regimen under Gargantua's new master,
Ponocrates, described in Chapters 23 and 24, is at every
point the reverse of what had gone before. Teaching starts
early in the morning, as soon as the pupil rises, and con-

tinues, in varied forms, throughout the day. It can do so
because the student is an active and eager participant,
not an inert recipient. A well-chosen and judiciously tem-
pered list of books are studied, never by rote memoriza-
tion but by explication and discussion, and the matter of
these books is the theme of conversation during meals and
on walks. There is music. There is horsemanship and
swimming and other active sports. Formal lectures are
attended only when the weather is bad. There are "field
trips" to various kinds of workshops and to establishments
where herbs and other curiosities are sold. There are
pleasant excursions to the country, but on these the talk
would be of the *Georgics* and Hesiod, as there was always
good talk at meals and pastimes. What comes to the Hel-
lenist's mind is the description of the old-fashioned education put into the mouth of Just Reason in the debate in
Aristophanes' *Clouds,* and in particular the closing lines:

> *But you will below to the Academe go, and under*
> *   the olives contend*
> *With your chaplet of reed, in a contest of speed*
> *   with some excellent rival and friend:*
> *'All fragrant with woodbine and peaceful con-*
> *   tent, and the leaf which the lime blossoms*
> *   fling,*
> *When the plane whispers love to the elm in the*
> *   grove in the beautiful season of Spring.*

The upshot is that when Gargantua had unlearned the old
ways, he enjoyed the tautened sinews of body and mind,

and enjoyed having his curiosity whetted and nourished. Man by nature desires to know, and learning is fun.

The implications of rational education for new views of man and society are given at large in the account of the establishment of the Abbey of Thélème, which occupies Chapters 53-58. The constitution of Thélème, is not only the heart of Rabelais' doctrine: it is an epitome of the new humanist outlook upon the nature of man. The design for the Abbey is simple enough: Rabelais merely reverses the usages of traditional abbeys. The motto for Rabelais' establishment, which is in effect a coeducational finishing school, is "Do what thou wilt," and at every point the severe prescriptions of the ordinary abbey, which are calculated to prevent a man from doing what he naturally would, are systematically nullified. Where ordinary abbeys are dank and forbidding, Thélème is sunny and attractive. The rigid schedule of hours is totally abolished, for clocks are banished from the abbey. Instead of drab and uniform habits, dress is colorful and elegant and varied, and instead of segregation of sexes, men and women are encouraged to associate freely. Where the system represented by ordinary abbeys premises the natural depravity of man, who can rise only by strenuous and directed efforts, the Abbey of Thélème is premised upon the natural goodness of man, in whom corruption is caused by the constraints of the world about him. If the causes of distortion are eliminated and the nature of man is allowed to assert itself freely, it will bloom and attain its proper excellence. It is the function of education not to check the natural development but to facilitate and encourage it. This, the sixteenth-century humanists believed, could best be done by studying the ancient humanists, who supplied material and direction for their enterprise; and those who agree with the position of the humanists will find that the Greeks can still provide material and direction.

Montaigne is not so slashing in his condemnation of the old, nor yet so much the *enfant terrible* in his advocacy of the new. Indeed the great charm of Montaigne is his urbanity; his innovations seem reasonable because he does not shriek and wave flags to call attention to them. His essay *On Pedantry* does with a smile what Rabelais had done with a roar. His *Apology for Raimond Sebonde,* his essay *On Cannibals* and his *On Education,* and indeed all his writings are premised on the assumption that the proper goal for education is humanity, not rejection of humanity and assimilation to an extra-human ideal. His account of his own education, which involved Latin-speaking servants, being awakened by music and other amenities, makes clear his belief that the personality of the pupil should be respected and fostered, that the pupil should not be forcibly fed with distasteful materials to be learned by rote. Actually Plutarch, who was one of Montaigne's two favorite authors (the other was Seneca) says much the same things in his *On the Education of Children;* but these things have had to be said again periodically, and are periodically received as new revelation.

For the education of educators, the proper agents, at least in humanist society, were the literary critics and theorists, who dictated how books should be written. Two merit a brief mention in this place, if only to correct misapprehensions. The first is Hieronymus Vida (1490-1566), whose *Art of Poetry* was enormously influential. John Milton called him "Cremona's Trump," and Alexander Pope hailed him in laudatory terms:

> Hail, light of Italy, thou brightest of the bards! Thee we worship, thee we adore with wreaths, with frankincense, with altars; to thee, as duty bids, for everlasting will we chaunt our holy hymns. Hail, consecrated bard! No increase to thy glory flows from praise, nor needs it voice of ours. Be near, and look upon thy votaries; come, father, and infuse thy fervor into our chaste hearts, and plant thyself within our souls.

The sum of the teaching in Vida's *Poetics* is that Vergil must be the sole model for all who would write poetry, and the fact is frequently cited to show the deadening influence of intransigent classicism. Vida's own *Christiad* is regularly dismissed as an empty cento of Vergilian tags. There are of course Vergilian expressions and rhythms, but these are used to fashion a quite independent poem with its own outlook and its own majesty. Even in Vida the classical ideal implies ideals of excellence, and modes of attaining it which should be emulated, not a pattern for copying.

Julius Caesar Scaliger (1484–1558) who taught at Leyden is much better known than Vida, possibly because he was more copious, more irascible, and more arrogant. His greatest work is his enormous *Poetics* in seven books and 944 pages. His whole concern is of course with the classics, and his criticism is judicious as well as learned. But Scaliger himself is the best evidence that preoccupation with the classics did not imply servitude but could encourage independence. "The Greeks are mistaken," Scaliger says, "if they think we have taken anything from them except to improve it." Earlier critics he brushes away cavalierly, not only Vida, but also Aristotle and Horace. What the many writers who studied Scaliger learned was not only to know the classics but to go beyond them.

VIII
INTEGRATION

CULTURAL history is after all a stream, and there is nothing in its later reaches for which some germ cannot be found in the earlier. Sometimes for long stretches the stream is reduced to a feeble and unchanging trickle, sometimes it takes a sharp bend or swells into a torrent. It is the bends and torrents, of course, that are interesting and instructive. The most fruitful of all, for us, is the Renaissance of which I have been speaking, for it was out of the new insights and interests then engendered that our own familiar world took shape. What produced the Renaissance was essentially an educational process, promoted by teachers. What facilitated its spread to embrace all Europeans was a reform in the practices of education and an enlargement of education's scope, both in its content and in its public. I should like now to say something of the ways in which the new education first colored and then dominated and then was assimilated into the general cultural stream.

The basis for the whole movement, clearly and unequivocally, were the literary works surviving from antiquity. To be sure, these works had never been wholly

forgotten; Dante, who was not an heir but rather a pro-
genitor of the Renaissance, affords sufficient proof that
they had been continuously operative. The learned Eloise
knew as many pagan books as her Abelard, and was visibly
influenced by them. Even the new outlooks which are
commonly said to be the products of the Renaissance—a
concern with this world rather than another, freedom instead of constraint for intellectual exploration, a bias in
favor of pleasure instead of suspicion of it, an assertion
of the dignity of man instead of an unremitting effort to
assimilate man to an ideal outside humanity—the ferment
which led to all of these had begun to stir before the revival of ancient books, and indeed motivated the revival.
What the revival did was to articulate the ferment, provide it with patterns and with authority, and give it definite
shape and direction.

The operational effectiveness of the revived books can
profitably be separated into stages: discovery and appreciation of the qualities of the ancient literature and acceler-
ated propagation of the new knowledge; translation into
vernaculars; vernacular imitations of classical works; more
original emulation of the classical models; assimilation so
complete that the patterns are no longer easily discernible
but are nevertheless so central that the new work could
never have been produced without them. A convenient
laboratory specimen for illustrating the successive stages
is the drama in Renaissance Italy, which is a highly artificial form created solely out of ancient models with no
admixture of non-classical elements. The beginnings of
the more powerful drama in England and Spain will not
serve so well because in addition to the classical materials

and, more important, classical impulse learned from the Italians, these two national dramas contained local ingredients also. The latter also, it may be noted, may have been ultimately of Greek derivation: Hamlet is surely Orestes, after he had undergone vicissitudes in northerly climates and had been given the shape Shakespeare knew by Saxo Grammaticus.

The doors were opened with the recognition that the books were originally intended for a public to read, not as a reserve for clerks. When the introduction of the Humanities course, of which I have spoken in an earlier chapter, was mooted in my own college, the strongest opposition came from clerkly teachers who could not tolerate the thought that a text which they could never cover in a year would be trampled over in a week. But the introduction of the Humanities program resulted in a much wider and, frequently, a much more intelligent appreciation of the books as books; and so it was in the Renaissance also. When books came to be regarded as books instead of esoteric mysteries, their high art came to be recognized. In the sixth century Gregory, who deserved his appellation "the Great" both as administrator and as churchman, decried attention to grammar and style. "The praises of Christ cannot be pronounced by the same lips as the praises of Jove," he said, and, "It is altogether inappropriate to keep the language of the Divine Oracles in subjection to the rules of Donatus." To return to the genre I have chosen as specimen, in the tenth century the nun, Hrostwitha of Gandersheim, wrote a series of pious plays following the models of Terence, but without realizing that Terence's were in verse. Her deviations from classical language, she says, were intentional. It should be remarked that both Hrostwitha and her plays are under suspicion of being fabrications by scholarly pranksters of the Humanist age; we know of no other attempt to imitate ancient plays between antiquity and the Renaissance.

That drama was in fact a noble art form, elaborately organized and skilfully executed by mature artists of the highest standing and worthy of the serious attention of intelligent audiences, was the principal lesson which the Renaissance learned from ancient drama; that is why they would not adulterate their new efforts with the relics of the vulgar performances directed to the mob. The same lesson of form is apparent in other genres also, most notably perhaps in the prose romances of the Greeks. To readers bred on the amorphous and almost infinite romances such as Don Quixote's housekeeper and curate burned, it was a revelation to see that an intricate plot could be artistically organized with beginning, middle, and end. Indeed it was the form of the ancient works that most attracted the Italians; to the profound spiritual probings we find in Greek tragedy, they seem to have been blind. They understood Roman comedy well enough, and imitated it skilfully, and they were impressed with the rhetoric and the intensity of Seneca. They thought, not unnaturally in view of its character, that tragedy was meant to be sung, and it was by reason of this misunderstanding that they invented opera.

The clearest proof that the brilliant culture characteristic of the Renaissance derived from the new interest in ancient books, is the theater. Late in the fifteenth century the *De Architectura* of Vitruvius, a Roman architect of

the age of Augustus, was discovered, and it was with
Vitruvius' difficult section on theater construction in hand
that Renaissance architects built their theaters, notably
the Teatro Olimpico at Vicenza. Actually the theaters they
built were obviously more like our own than like the ancient Romans'—for one thing they were enclosed within
a palace building rather than open-air—just as their "tragedies" were more like what is presented at the Metropolitan
Opera House than at the Theater of Dionysus at Athens.
But in one case as in the other the result was innovation,
in real or fancied continuation of ancient practice, not a
development of what had gone before.

Attempts to act out ancient Latin plays, or new ones
written in imitation of the ancient, were naturally limited
to small and select audiences, but were nevertheless en-
larging; the two written by Buchanan at Bordeaux, which
I have spoken of, were serious and thought-provoking
works of art. Similarly in epic, Petrarch's *Africa,* which is
little more than a stunt, eventually gives way to a work
like Vida's *Christiad,* which is literature. The audience for
Latin works became larger and more critical. Valla's intro-
ductions to his excellent Latin versions of Herodotus and
Thucydides have a legitimate claim not only as illuminat-
ing scholarship but also as literature. Of original literary
works in Latin, informed by study of the ancients but not
copying them, such as Erasmus' *Colloquies* or More's
Utopia, I have spoken above.

What made the spread of books possible, and multiplied
demand for them, was of course the invention of printing.
The productions of the Aldine Press at Venice in particular
were excellent in scholarship, beautiful in execution, and

cheap in price; one papal license granted Aldus stipulates that prices must be kept moderate. The only adequate parallel to the sudden and enormous expansion of audiences is that effected by the mass media of communication, especially radio and television, in our day. A professed humanist may be pardoned his conviction that the Aldines were more sincerely and more effectively concerned for standards of quality and taste than are our broadcasters; for one thing, conscientious and competent critics—a Scaliger, for example—were effective guardians of standards. But a humanist may also believe that, in concerns of the spirit, Gresham's Law need not apply; very soon the audience itself must develop articulate and critical sense, and the bad will yield to the good.

The next step is translation, inevitably so in view of the enlarged public, and desirably so. Because a teacher of Greek and Latin is expected to deplore the use of translations, I must say at once that I believe profoundly that they are a good thing; how I arrived at this belief, in defiance of my own teachers, and why I hold it so firmly, I shall set forth in my closing chapter. Here I wish to remark that the activity itself, not alone the product in the shape of a book which is made accessible to millions instead of hundreds, is a highly desirable and efficient humanistic enterprise. If Isocrates was right, as he indubitably was, in regarding *logos* as the essential quality of humanity, if it is impossible to have a thought about anything at all, without the use of words and verbal relationships, then it is important, in order to deal with rich and complex thoughts with precision and with taste, to know what we can about *logos*. The best means to this end, I am convinced, is the practice of translation. There is no surer way of detecting turgidity and illogicality in a piece of English than by trying to put it into Latin, no surer way of sensing refinements and overtones in a piece of Greek than by trying to put it into English. It was to attain perceptions of this sort, and not merely for drill in grammatical forms, that Roger Ascham's *Scholemaster* repeatedly insists upon translation and retranslation as the proper technique for education.

It might have been better, for preserving the unity of Europe, if Erasmus had succeeded in making Latin its common language, but we can see, in retrospect, that the hope was visionary. What the hope was basically intended to achieve, a common store of *logoi* which all Europe could share, was achieved by translation. All of us know (or, more realistically, can know) the Bible and the Greeks and the Romans, Dante and Montaigne, Cervantes and Shakespeare, Goethe and Tolstoy. The effects of translation go far beyond spreading *logoi* in the larger sense; translations enlarge the mind in subtler ways also. The translation of the Greek Bible called the Septuagint, for instance, which has doubtless been the most influential of all translations, meant to give a precise version of the Hebrew, and quite correctly rendered the Hebrew word for soul (*neshamah*) by its Greek equivalent (*psyche*). But *psyche* carried a crowd of implications, alien to the Hebrew, which generations of Greek philosophers had elaborated, and our "soul" retains those connotations. Through the version of the Bible called King James', in turn, a crowd of

Hebrew images and outlooks have been naturalized into English. It is through translation, in a word, that disparate skeins are woven into a single and universal texture.

Humanist translators of Greek and Latin not only made the ancient books accessible but were, like Falstaff, the cause of wit in others. Possibly the greatest of all translators is the Frenchman Jacques Amyot (1513-1593), whose versions are as scholarly as they are artistic. It was to Amyot, "who made Plutarch speak French," that Montaigne owed his familiarity with that author, as he gratefully acknowledges, and it was Amyot's version of the *Lives* that Thomas North turned into English and made accessible to Shakespeare. Shakespeare knew Ovid through Arthur Golding's version of the *Metamorphoses*. George Chapman's loud and bold version of Homer could still make Keats feel like stout Cortez. Chapman also completed the version of Musaeus' *Hero and Leander* which Christopher Marlowe had left unfinished. Marlowe's own versions of Ovid's *Amores* and of the first book of Lucan are masterly. By the end of the sixteenth century enough of the classics were available in translation, on the continent as well as in England, to make knowledge of them common among all literate people. One other English version should be mentioned, in order to get back to our dramatic thread, and that is the *Tenne Tragedies of Seneca* by various hands (1581), which was a major factor in giving Elizabethan tragedy its contours.

After literal translation comes adaptation, which is peculiarly common and effective in drama. Usually the main outlines of the plot and the *dramatis personae* are retained; changes are in the direction of conformity with current

habits and outlooks. The comedies of Plautus and Terence
are themselves adaptations of the Greek New Comedy of
Menander and his rivals, and the Romans in turn were
adapted in all the languages of Europe. Italian production
in this kind was first and most voluminous, but the practice
quickly spread. Shakespeare's *Comedy of Errors* is an
adaptation of Plautus' *Menaechmi,* Molière's *L'Avare* of
Plautus' *Aulularia,* Ben Jonson's *The Case is Altered* a
conflation of Plautus' *Aulularia* and *Captivi.* The list can
be multiplied tenfold. Adaptations of tragedy are later and
tend to deviate more from their models. A "classical" tragedy like Racine's *Phèdre* will follow Seneca or Euripides
closely for a considerable space and then take a turn the
ancients could not have imagined. An extreme example in
this kind is Goethe's *Iphigenie auf Tauris;* the plot and
dramatis personae are Euripides', the use of verse is in ac-
cordance with ancient practice, but the Christian and romantic coloring of the relationship between the Greek prin-
cess and the barbarian king is different from anything the
Greeks could conceive—and surely also inferior.

There has been a marked revival of adaptations of ancient plays in the twentieth century, especially in the hands
of French playwrights like Giraudoux or Anouilh. Here the
form is less faithful to the ancients but the content con-
spicuously more so. Basic to the conception of Greek
tragedy, and what gives the Greek plays their profundity,
is the struggle between two exigent sanctions, each of which
has validity and each of which has power to punish. Where
one code of conduct is wholly approved and the other
wholly condemned there can be no tragedy of the Greek
type but only melodrama, edifying when the hero prevails

and the villain is crushed, or shocking if the issue is reversed. The twentieth-century adaptations are closer to the Greek because they, too, acknowledge the validity of more than one sanction for conduct. The Renaissance did indeed take up where the ancients left off, but it was very far from taking up and ingesting *all* that the ancients had done and thought. The process which the Renaissance initiated continues; the ancients are still capable of furnishing new directions and new insights.

Along with adaptation comes imitation, in which plot and *dramatis personae* are invented instead of borrowed, but where technique, atmosphere, and moral are clearly informed by the ancients. The pioneers in this kind were again the Italians, and especially Ariosto, in whom we can see adaptation growing freer until new works, but similar to the old in kind, are produced. A play like Machiavelli's *Mandragola* is thoroughly contemporary but also manifestly an imitation of the ancient Romans. Molière's *Les Fourberies de Scapin* is less obviously Terence's *Phormio* than his *L'Avare* is Plautus' *Aulularia;* the *Misanthrope* and the rest are the same in kind and show unmistakable touches of Plautus and Terence, but they are imitations rather than adaptations. *Volpone* and the *Alchemist* have a kinship with *The Case is Altered* but are independent plays. Restoration comedy makes new and different drafts upon the Romans; its Fop, for example, is a direct descendant of the Braggart Soldier type of the ancients.

Another category includes plays which are not imitations but in which plots and *dramatis personae* come from the ancient books. This is a frank kind of emulation. Shakespeare's Roman plays—*Julius Caesar, Anthony and Cleo-*

patra, Coriolanus—are based on Plutarch. The dramatic
pages of Tacitus' history have suggested many plays; Cor-
neille has an *Otho,* Racine a *Britannicus,* Ben Jonson a
Sejanus, Alfieri an *Octavia,* Chénier a *Tiberius,* and there
are a dozen plays on Nero. As in other respects our own
generation prefers the Greeks; Giraudoux' *The Trojan War
Will Not Take Place,* for instance, which has proved a success in English under the title *Tiger at the Gates,* goes
back to the Homeric milieu.

Far more important than adaptation or conscious imitation or the kind of emulation which advertises its exploitation by the use of classical names and classical setting, is
the kind of emulation which is tacit, and more important
still is the kind in which the author himself may be un-
aware of his indebtedness. Surely without the model of
Seneca, Marlowe would not have invented his overreach-
ing characters, would not have endowed them with such
titanic and obsessive passions, or put such gorgeous rhetoric
into their mouths; and Marlowe was doubtless aware of his
indebtedness. Shakespeare may not have been, but he
would not have written his drama in verse, would not have
favored classical names, would not have been concerned
with stark passions if Seneca had not written, as Seneca
would not have if the Greeks had not. There is no reason
why great creative artists like Aeschylus and Shakespeare
could not have invented a Clytemnestra and a Lady Macbeth independently. But it happens that these two very
similar creations are in fact one: Lady Macbeth is Clytemnestra in Elizabethan dress.

I must take the time to explain how I became persuaded
that this is so, for the discovery of the relationship is the

kind of thing which is peculiarly gratifying to a bookish man and is germane to the subject of the chapter. Some years ago, in connection with a study of Livy, I was examining certain later historians to see how they might have been influenced by him. A major object of Livy's early books (as of Vergil's *Aeneid*) was to show that the Romans were an elect, destined to fulfil a high destiny. The *Historia Scotorum* of Hector Boece, published in 1527, was similarly motivated to show that the Scots are God's chosen. Boece not only learned from Livy's general outlook and techniques but frequently adapted considerable stretches of Livy's prose. Where Boece tells of the murder of Duncan by Macbeth and his Lady, in his tenth book, he must clearly have had Livy's story of the murder of Servius by his ambitious daughter and her husband before him, as the close similarity of phrasing proves. Livy, in turn, must surely have had a Greek tragedy, and specifically a version of Aeschylus' *Agamemnon,* in mind. He introduces the story with the sentence, "Roman history too produced an example of tragic crime" and "tragic" did not yet mean "shocking" or "sad" but referred specifically to drama. His story sounds like the résumé of a tragic plot, and even speaks of avenging Furies. We know that Accius' *Clutemestra,* which was an adaptation of the *Agamemnon,* was acted in Rome in the first century B.C. There is considerable probability, therefore, that Boece's story of the Macbeths derives ultimately from Aeschylus. But were there not versions of the story other than Boece's which Shakespeare might have used? The other versions do not make Lady Macbeth the powerful instigator of the crime, as Boece does; Holinshed's version must depend on Boece, and

Shakespeare drew from Holinshed. Not only plays whose *dramatis personae* are historical ancient worthies like Caesar or Coriolanus, but those with British setting have been substantially shaped by the classical tradition. Here the tradition is fully integrated.

But though the exotic classical tradition had been assimilated to create a new and native drama, the tradition itself continued operative. Sometimes it has been followed with scrupulous pedantry, as in Matthew Arnold's *Merope*. Here Arnold apparently sought to give a Greekless public the closest possible approximation of a Greek tragedy, and on a Greek theme, but in verse superior to that of contemporary translations of real Greek tragedy. *Merope* is indeed a skilful exercise, but it is not a Greek drama. Far more successful, and indeed superior to any "Greek" tragedy written after the Greeks (which includes Seneca's), is the *Samson Agonistes* of John Milton. Here the theme is drawn from Scripture rather than Greek myth, but if a Greek audience were informed of the story of Samson, one feels, it would find Milton's play intelligible and meaningful as it could never find adaptations of Greek tragedy by Racine or Goethe. Milton's understanding of what the Greeks were about is evident throughout the *Samson* and not least in its concluding phrase, "with new acquist of true experience all passion spent."

Drama composed for a living theater aims to entertain a large and heterogeneous contemporary audience, with little thought of an eventual reading public. It is otherwise with works which are meant to be read by a bookish public and which are expected to survive into a remote future.

The later ancients and later ages which accepted their ideals believed that the noblest of all achievements possible for mortal man was the authorship of an epic poem. There are scholars who believe that the authors of *Roland* and the *Cid,* even of *Beowulf* and *Nibelungenlied,* must have known Vergil, but the matter is of no great consequence; the sophisticated writers of post-Renaissance epic did not model themselves upon them. All of these, and especially such somber and serious artists as Tasso or Camoens or John Milton, not only knew Vergil but assumed that their audiences would know him and exploited this knowledge. This mode of acclimatizing the ancients is one no longer commonly practised, and hence a few words should be said about it.

Neither Camoens, whose *Lusiads* (published in 1572) is the epic of Portugal, nor John Milton in his *Paradise Lost,* made a secret of their emulation of the ancients; indeed they overtly invite comparison with them. Camoens advertises the emulation in his Vergilian opening:

Arms and those matchless chiefs . . .
My song shall sow through the world's every part.

His own project is more serious:

Of the wise Greek no more the tale unfold,
Or the Trojan, and great voyages they made . . .
I sing the Lusian spirit bright and bold,
That Mars and Neptune equally obeyed.

> Forget all the Muse sang in ancient days,
> For valor nobler yet is now to praise.

As we shall presently see, Camoens counts on his readers
not to forget all the Muse sang in ancient days.

Milton is as explicit:

> Sad task, yet argument
> Not less but more Heroic than the wrauth
> Of stern *Achilles* on his Foe pursu'd
> Thrice Fugitive about *Troy* Wall; or rage
> Of Turnus for *Lavinia* disespous'd
> Or *Neptun's* ire or *Juno's,* that so long
> Perplex'd the *Greek* and *Cytherea's* Son.

Camoen's immediate theme is the voyage of the Portuguese under Vasco da Gama around the continent of Africa and on to India. He starts, as Vergil does, with the
fleet caught in a storm near the end of the voyage and pre-
sents the antecedent events and the history of Portugal,
past and in prospect, through flashbacks contrived like
Vergil's. His larger theme, like Vergil's, is the destiny of
an elect—all Christendom represented by the Portuguese
—against the undisciplined and hostile forces of barbary.
The Portuguese are represented as the logical successors
of the Romans (even their language is an obvious development from Latin) destined to carry the Roman task forward to higher goals. As in Vergil each party has its patron
deity; the East's is now not Juno but Bacchus, who is an
appropriate representative for the capricious and slippery
easterners.

But it is not merely for framework, epic machinery, patriotic objectives that Camoens emulated Vergil. Throughout his poem episodes, expressions, images are unmistakably reminiscent of parallels in Vergil, but each is different in some significant way. The poet is then not merely decorating his structure with borrowed and meretricious finery, but increasing his resources for communication. The reader who remembers the Vergilian pattern himself constructs a kind of counterpoint between what Camoens is saying and what Vergil said. New dimensions are added in the most economical and hence most effective way. The mere substitution of a daisy for a Vergilian poppy, for example, suggests a contrast between a pagan and a Christian climate of thought.

John Milton (who alludes to Camoens' poem) is more obtrusively learned; in effect he demands his reader's academic credentials before he will admit him to his *Paradise Lost*. It is easy to say and of course true that the Latinate style of *Paradise Lost* and its rich bookish allusiveness are the natural mode of expression for a poet so erudite as Milton; but that is not the sum of the matter. He might well have dispensed with reminders of the ancients but deliberately chose to use them, even the striking inversions of word order which he does not use in other poems, for ends like Camoens'. The effect is intentionally polysemous. The words carry with them not only their surface meanings but also corollary clouds which serve to elaborate, contrast, expound.

What is important for us is the ultimate result. The enrichment, which is a kind of attached increment in its first use, becomes absorbed into the texture of poesy, and the fused meanings go onward as an inseparable and independent entity. Disparate *logoi* become a larger and richer *logos*. That is how the study of the classics enriched *logoi* for the Greeks, and that is how study of the classics can still enrich *logoi* for us.

IX

NO TRESPASSING

F<small>ULLY</small> as the products of the revival of ancient books were integrated into the main streams of vernacular culture in the countries of Europe, the ancient books themselves retained their own independent being, their high esteem, and their central position as the subject matter of education. The program of education in the humanistic age and after, indeed the actual curriculum, was not essentially different from what it had been in antiquity. *Didaskalos,* the ordinary Greek word for teacher, means, unless it is specifically otherwise qualified, a teacher of reading and books, and, as I have noted in my second chapter, the books that were taught, whether in old Greece or in areas newly Hellenized, were the classics. In Rome, similarly, the teacher beyond the elementary level was called *grammaticus,* and what he taught was literature. It was because Livius Andronicus, who served as a *grammaticus* in Rome in the third century B.C., had no suitable Latin classics to use in his work that he translated the *Odyssey* into Latin.

Modern educators who demonstrate their modernity by constant devices for "enrichment" are naturally shocked

at the narrowness of such a curriculum, and with some justification. But a glance at some of the textbooks used in the
process might soften the shock somewhat. I have looked
over a half-dozen made by Charles Anthon, one of my
predecessors at Columbia, before his death in 1867. A text
of Horace's *Odes,* for example, which can be printed in
fewer than a hundred pages, occupies a thousand. At the
top of each page runs a thin trickle of two or three lines
of Horace, and this is supported by two stout columns of
commentary in tiny type. For construing the Latin the commentary offers no more, if as much, help as strictly dieted
modern texts do; what takes up the space are remarks on a
wide variety of subjects attached to the Latin in hand by
webs so tenuous as to be scarcely visible. All that Anthon's
well-stocked mind contained on every subject that might interest a gentleman is put into the commentary for the education of his students, just as his own rich stock had doubtless been largely acquired in a course labelled Latin. So
conceived a course in a classical author is not a subject but
a curriculum, and the curious and industrious student subjected to such a course may have emerged as well informed,
in subjects appropriate to the Liberal Arts, as his modern
successors are. Particularization of subject matter, carried
to the extreme from which we are only now retreating, can
produce cross-sterilization as well as cross-fertilization.

The crux of the matter is the word "gentleman" which I
have used above. The gentlemanly ideal permeated the
whole system, to a large extent in Greece, to a larger in
Rome, and with even more class consciousness in England.
The concept of "gentleman", for which the English word

has been adopted by the other languages of Europe, goes back to Baldassare Castiglione's *Book of the Courtier,* of which Hoby's translation (1561) was extremely influential. Dr. Johnson called it "the best book that ever was written upon good breedings." Castiglione's own views with regard to education are unexceptionable. He remarks that in France noblemen did not consider reading books a respectable occupation and himself prescribes reading, along with music, dancing, and athletics, as essential for the courtier. But the gentlemanly ideal, which included education in the classics, was too brittle a thing to survive intact in a rising democracy. In the first place the mere association of classical education with social snobbery, and the fact that such education was flaunted as a badge of gentlemanly standing, was enough to discredit it in a society growing increasingly egalitarian. In the second place the books upon which the education was centered were believed to preserve and inculcate views which the egalitarians found objectionable.

Even today people whose true commitment lies elsewhere advocate and support the old education not for the humanist's reasons, indeed to his acute discomfort, but because they believe that such education will preserve the generally conservative religious or political and social outlooks they cherish. I have heard the professor in charge of undergraduate work in the Humanities in a major eastern university declare that the only valid reason for studying the Humanities was as a *Praeparatio Evangelica* (the phrase, which means "Preparation for the Gospel," is the title of a work by the Church historian Eusebius). And I have heard classical education defended as a prophylactic against subversiveness. Advocacy of humanistic education on such grounds is of course mistaken both in practice and in theory. Study of the classics does not in fact bolster orthodoxy either religious or political, and the proper use of such study is not to reinforce existing prejudices, however true and desirable, but to explore, without necessarily adopting, outlooks which are less familiar, to stretch the mind, not to curb its elasticity.

But the motives of More and Colet and Grocyn, of Ascham and Elyot, and their thousand successors who established classical education as the norm in England, cannot be questioned; there have never been wanting, and there never will be, men whose love of learning and love of teaching are wholly pure. However we assay the motives of the others, the fact remains that in England, as on the continent and in the colonies, education meant classical education. It was because education par excellence meant classical education that, as it turned out, a knowledge of Greek seemed the normal prerequisite for preferment in state as in church. But in view of the distinction I have drawn between the knightly education and the scribal, it must be said that the posture of classical education in England was predominantly of the knightly type. It was relatively recently, for example, that Latin was introduced as a subject for university study—every boy was expected to have learned it before university age as he learned English, at his mother's knee, it has been said, and other low joints. University study, where few attend universities, implies the scribe.

There were, indeed, virtuoso scholars: one need only mention Richard Bentley (1662–1742) who was Europe's greatest. Aside from his pioneer work in the science of textual criticism and his brilliant hypothesis concerning the Greek digamma, Bentley's great achievement was his exposure of certain highly regarded works as forgeries, in his *Dissertation Upon the Epistles of Phalaris.* The significant thing here, for our present purposes, is that interest in the *Dissertation* was not, as would be the case today, limited to Bentley's own guild of scholars; every literate person was interested in the subject, and several of the foremost writers of the day (not professional scholars) wrote books and pamphlets supporting or impugning Bentley's positions. The writers were themselves well informed, and what is more significant, could expect that their readers (not students) would also be well informed.

Evidence of easy familiarity with the classics is shown by all of English literature, almost, if not quite, to the present. A speaker in Parliament could start a line in an ancient poet and feel sure his audience could complete it. A writer could cite apposite quotations in the ancient languages and feel no need to translate. Within the year I have seen a discussion of President Hoover's administration in a British periodical of general circulation in which the phrase *consensu omnium capax,* "by general consent competent," was used, apparently with perfect confidence that the reader would supply Tacitus' conclusion of the sentence, *imperii nisi imperasset,* "to rule if he had not in fact ruled." A man could put an inscription or dedication in an ancient language without fear of being thought pretentious. The change which has taken place was brought home to me a few years ago by a personal experience with the late Justice Cardozo, whose memory I cherish. Judge Cardozo, who read Greek for pleasure, had been given the task of editing a volume in honor of his senior colleague, Justice Holmes, and had picked as a suitable motto for the dedicatory page, lines spoken of Achilles in Euripides' *Iphigenia at Aulis:*

> How can I praise thee, and not overpraise,
> And yet not mar the grace by stint thereof?

Judge Cardozo had decided to print the translation because he feared printing the Greek would look pretentious; I am glad that I was able to persuade him that Judge Holmes would be more honored if Euripides' own language were used. If the volume were not addressed to a particular individual, but intended for the public at large, I am not sure I would have tried to be so persuasive. The fact is that a display of Greek has become somewhat precious, like wearing gloves when the weather does not demand them. I must now say why I think the change has come about.

It was about the beginning of the nineteenth century that two directions in classical study, both emanating from Germany, resulted in the gradual withdrawal of classical knowledge from the realm of the generally familiar and its relegation to an esoteric preserve, marked, as it were, with a No Trespassing sign. The impulse for both movements may be derived, with something of oversimplification, from the good and useful work of two outstanding scholars—J. J. Winckelmann (1717–1768), whose principal work was *Geschichte der Kunst des Altertums,* and F. A. Wolf (1750–1824), whose principal work was *Prolegomena ad Homerum.* Winckelmann studied and understood the aesthetics of ancient sculpture as no one had done

before. His perceptive taste enabled him to distinguish orig-
inals from copies, Greek work from Roman, early from
late, to classify works by periods, and to show the artistic
ideals and techniques appropriate to each period. Winckelmann's observations were correct and his inferences sound.
His work has of course been elaborated, corrected, and refined, but remains essentially sound; all who deal with ancient sculpture have learned from him.

Wolf's *Prolegomena* similarly approached the Homeric
poems as artistic productions—and on that basis found
them wanting. The construction of the poems Wolf found
faulty, with some portions different from others in scale,
cultural level, and outlook. The discrepancies and incon-
cinnities were due, Wolf argued, to the fact that the poems
were not unitary productions of a single author, but actually a series of disparate lays of diverse date and authorship which had been "stitched" together (*rhapsode* may
mean "stitcher of songs") under the patronage of Pisi-
stratus, tyrant of Athens. Wolf's most telling argument, almost universally accepted during the nineteenth century,
was that poems so long could be composed only in writing,
and that writing was not known in Greece at the presumed
date of the composition of the Homeric poems.

Both parts of Wolf's argument have been refuted in the
present century. The researches of Milman Parry and others, working with techniques of oral composition mainly
among the Jugoslavs, have shown that poems longer than
Iliad and *Odyssey* can in fact be composed orally, by bards
who cannot read or write. And Michael Ventris has shown,
through the decipherment of Minoan Linear B inscriptions
on clay tablets in Crete, that people in the Aegean could

in fact write Greek hundreds of years before the presumed date of composition of the Homeric poems. Now conservative opinion agrees that the techniques of the poems do indubitably follow the modes of oral composition, but that the actual poems were composed in writing, probably both by the poet called Homer, but in any case each by an individual poet. Not Wolf's hypothesis alone, but the prodigious mass of ingenious scholarship based upon it, has been discredited. And yet Wolf's work was by no means without fruit. The new life it infused into Homeric study sharpened the study of other classical texts also, the method came to be applied to other traditional monuments, including the Bible, and the conviction that epics were composite gave Elias Lönnrot the idea of fashioning the Finnish "epic" called *Kalevala* out of separate scattered lays.

If men like Winckelmann and Wolf generated our impulse towards a more mature and precise appreciation of the classical heritage, the extreme to which the impulse was carried in some directions served to constrict, rather than enlarge, the range of interest, and to exclude all but professionals from participation in the heritage. Friedrich von Schlegel (1772–1829) set out to do with Greek literature what Winckelmann had done with Greek art. The schemes he constructed were based solely on aesthetic perceptions, sometimes romantic and mystical in quality, and in any case subjective. But criteria which are convincing in sculpture are not so in poetry. Winckelmann could speak with some assurance of what must have been in the gaps of his unfilled scheme; Schlegel did so without basis (as when he categorizes Menander on the strength of isolated single-line quotations) and hence carries no conviction. But the main fault with criticism of Schlegel's type is that it leaves the rest of us happy in our Philistinism. Modern students of Greek tragedy may be guilty of a different distortion when they concentrate on the doctrine the tragic poets taught, on their dramaturgy, and on their subtle poetic techniques, but all the world is interested in doctrine and a good part of it in dramaturgy and poetic techniques. To view Sophocles as a bloodless marmoreal figure, concerned only with mystic beauty and turning the blank eyes of a Greek statue upon the world of passion, is unjust to Sophocles and unjust to his potential audience.

The essentially romantic views of Schlegel and his kind still survive in what earthlings like myself call the Olympian stance, and books on Sophocles still stress his marmoreal detachment. The best line-by-line commentary on the plays of Sophocles is probably that of Sir Richard Jebb, done in the years before and after 1900. A suggestion that a Sophoclean crisis or hero might be intended as a comment on some contemporary question or personality, Jebb finds shocking; it is a degradation of so pure an artist, he says, to think that he might have tainted his art with such ephemeral matters. But the classical poets looked upon themselves and were looked upon as responsible public teachers, who would be expected to speak out on important questions. They supplied a necessary commodity, and like other Greek craftsmen, say, makers of chairs, they strove to make their product as beautiful as possible. But who would make a chair, however beautiful, if it could not be sat upon? Art for art's sake is a doctrine wholly alien to classical Greece, and not very compelling in our own world.

If Greek poetry were art so pure, it would never have engaged the consuming attention of the Greeks, and it could never engage the consuming attention of other men. The view, initiated by Schlegel, that it is a remote and ethereal thing, has served in substantial measure to remove it from the ken of ordinary consumers of literature.

If the fault of the romantic approach is that it pointed a direction which the generality of men could not long follow, the fault of the scientific approach, for which Wolf's work was a point of departure, was that the direction it pointed led to a barred gate. The root of the trouble, if it can be localized, was the assumption that the study of antiquity must adopt the methods and aims of the exact sciences, which were then burgeoning. The goal was the establishment of truth, however inconsequential, for its own sake; any implications the truth might have for the fuller understanding of man were really incidental. With increasing specialization, disciplines within classical scholarship proliferated. At first there were two divergent schools, a "pure" grammatical and critical school, of which the leader was Gottfried Hermann (1768–1848), and an "applied" historical and antiquarian school, of which the leader was August Boeckh (1785–1867); between the two, literary understanding came near perishing. Soon, of course, each of the schools was further subdivided. The industry of nineteenth-century German scholarship was prodigious and its achievements amazing.

In the establishment of texts and in grammar, in history and archaeology, epigraphy and numismatics, in political and social and domestic institutions, the work of nineteenth-century German scholarship is permanently useful for the methods they laid down and for many of their conclusions. But laboratory study of the monuments of antiquity is rather less than more a liberation of the spirit than study of insects or stones. A distinguished philologist began his seminar on Sophocles' *Oedipus* by telling its members that they were highly privileged: the text they were to study contained more grammatical anomalies than any other. Another complained on his death bed that his career had been a failure because he had attempted too much: his mistake had been in choosing to study the dative case; if he had limited himself to one kind of dative, say the ethical, he might have achieved something. Browning depicts the type in his "Grammarian's Funeral":

> So, with the throttling hands of death at strife,
>   Ground he at grammar;
> Still, thro' the rattle, parts of speech were rife:
>   While he could stammer
> He settled *Hoti's* business—let it be!—
>   Properly based *Oun*—
> Gave us the doctrine of the enclitic *De*,
>   Dead from the waist down.

The assumption of nineteenth-century philologists, that finality is possible, shows both lack of imagination and arrogance. What those men studied, and by the methods they deemed correct, they studied with great success; but they could not conceive that there were other things to study in the classics or other methods of studying them. The business of the ethical dative could be despatched in a lifetime of work and a fat volume; when the business of all other datives and all other similar questions should be done, knowledge would be complete and could be entered, as a possession of unalterable validity as well as accuracy, in a large encyclopedia. Contemporary scholars have no such assurance of the finality of their work.

Scholarship so technical could obviously have no room for laymen. Anyone who sought to make the new knowledge accessible to the laity was suspect to the esoteric, and anyone who could write readable prose forfeited his standing as a scholar. A clairvoyant intellect like the Swiss Jakob Burckhardt was scorned by the professionals; his four-volume *Griechische Kulturgeschichte* remains the most sensible, informing, and attractive description of the totality of Greek civilization accessible to the layman, whereas his professional contemporaries are forgotten. It took courage for Mommsen to acknowledge that Renan was a scholar "even though he can write."

Professional exclusiveness has happily been relaxed, but vestiges of it persist, as I can testify from personal experience. When I was invited, two or three years ago, to address a meeting of teachers on problems of teaching classics in translation, the distinguished scholar who introduced me informed the audience that I was a man who made translations, wrote popularizing interpretations, and even reviewed books in my field for newspapers; he plainly meant no unkindness, but just as plainly found it remarkable that the professor of Greek in a reputable university should stray so far from the traditional boundaries. About 1940, I published a study of the religion of Plutarch in a scholarly but nonclassical periodical, and was told by a senior colleague, who was also a warm friend, that I had done very wrong not to publish it in a classical periodical. When I realized that he was in earnest, I said, "But the classicists already know; this will interest other people and should be made available to them." "Your responsibility is to your own profession," my colleague said. C. W. K. was one of the most saintly and most charitable men I have known, but I cannot help feeling that withholding knowledge from people who might profit by it is want of charity.

Classical study continued to be called humanistic in German academies, but by its technical specialization and consequent exclusiveness, it abdicated its character as a humanity. Other countries resisted the new pattern and none went to the German extreme, but all were more or less affected. The French in particular never lost the art of *haute vulgarisation*. For the history of Greek literature, for example, the reference work indispensable to the scholar is that by Christ, Schmid, and Stählin, in some half dozen large volumes kept up to date by constant revision, in the series called "Iwan von Muller's Handbuch der Altertumswissenschaft," but Christ-Schmid is to be consulted, not read. The *Histoire de la littérature grecque* of Alfred and Maurice Croiset, in five volumes, though it is not nearly so exhaustive or fully documented nor, alas, kept up to date by revision, can be read with delight as well as confidence by any lover of literature.

Least touched by the scientific phantom were the English. Their knowledge of the ancient languages was precise and penetrating, and they rather scorned German heavy-handedness in this respect, as is shown by the jibe (I must quote loosely, from memory):

> The Germans in Greek
> Are far to seek,
> All but Hermann,
> And Hermann
> Is German.

In the study of the physical remains of antiquity, the British antedated the Germans by far. The Society of Dilettanti, established in 1733, fostered such sumptuous publications as Stuart and Revett's *The Antiquities of Athens Measured and Delineated* (1762–1816) and the epigraphical collection of Richard Chandler (1738–1810). Charles Townley (1737–1805) and Richard Payne Knight (1750–1824) gave their names to famous collections. Sir William Hamilton (1730–1803) reported early discoveries at Pompeii. The program of the Dilettanti was supported by the traveler and statesman Robert Wood (1717–1771), whose *Essay on the Genius and Writings of Homer, with a Comparative View of the Ancient and Present State of the Troade* influenced both Wolf and Goethe; Wood thought that writing was not introduced into Greece until 554 B.C. Provided we remember that the Gentlemen often defeat the Players at Lord's, Dilettanti is an excellent characterization of British scholarship. The best history of Greece is the twelve-volume work of George Grote (1794–1871), who was a banker. The best translators of the classics—Andrew Lang, the Earl of Derby, B. B. Rogers, and a dozen others, were not professional scholars. What humanism is essentially concerned with, after all, is the written word—*logoi;* this the British have never lost sight of. Until yesterday or the day before they were the humanists of the modern world.

It was British practices and attitudes, naturally, that were the controlling influence in colonial America. Education meant classical education. The founding fathers thought and comported themselves like toga-draped worthies out of the pages of Plutarch. Thomas Jefferson in particular was well-read in the classics, and his career shows evidence of the fact. "Capitol," "senate," "father of his country," even Greek façades on public buildings, are not archaisms but a classical element thoroughly naturalized. But when colleges were transformed into universities, graduate study of the classics was organized and prosecuted in the German pattern. Until the first world war, study in Germany was virtually mandatory for any classical scholar who aspired to higher teaching in America; four of my own teachers held degrees from German universities. Even when the leading strings were cut, the Germanic requirement of the Ph.D. degree persisted. The consequences of professionalization for the position of humanistic study in America I wish to leave for my final chapter. But I do sometimes think that it might have been better if we had let our growth evolve naturally out of its British antecedents; at least the British do not make a fetish of the Ph.D. degree, which, however useful it may now be and however naturalized, was still, in its beginnings, the sign manifest of professionalism.

X

AMERICAN RENASCENCE

To say that the classics were abolished from the curriculum by men who had studied them and then restored by men who had not is exaggeration, but it comes near enough truth to make the official guardians of the classical tradition uncomfortable. The sequence of ossification, revitalization, ossification, revitalization, is a phenomenon common to all spiritual concerns, and particularly noticeable in religion. Zeal tends to calcify into a rote ritualism, and is then revivified, to the chagrin and often against the opposition of the official priesthood, by a man from the desert who is not a member of the prophet's guild. The renewal, if it is effective, is then incorporated into the body of the tradition in charge of the priesthood, again hardens into spiritless routine, and again invites revivification at the hands of people who have no vested interests in the subject, to the discomfort of those who have.

Something of the kind has happened in the case of classical teaching; there was of course the great revivification at the Renaissance, and another at the end of the eighteenth century. Each rise was followed by a sinking; in America the sinking was hastened by a particular combination of circumstances. From the beginning, and especially in our older centers of culture, learning was highly regarded and teachers enjoyed something of the respect paid to ministers. A man did not lose status by teaching, and the distribution of talent among teachers was not markedly different than among other men.

But with so much that needed to be done in a new and expanding country where the explosive growth of commerce and industry offered large opportunities for men of energy, the serenity of the gentlemanly mode of eighteenth-century education could not long remain undisturbed. There was indeed more than the usual justification for the saying that "those who can, do; those who can't, teach." There was even philosophical rationalization for impatience with traditional learning. A landmark in educational theory in America is Ralph Waldo Emerson's Phi Beta Kappa address on "The American Scholar", delivered at Harvard in 1837. Here is a paragraph relevant to our theme:

The books of an older period will not fit this. Yet hence arises a great mischief. The sacredness which attaches to the act of creation, the act of thought, is transferred to the record. Instantly the book becomes noxious: the guide is a tyrant. The sluggish and perverted mind of the multitude having once received this book, stands upon it and makes an outcry if it is destroyed. Colleges are built on it. Meek young men grow up in libraries. Hence, instead of men thinking, we have the bookworm. I had better never see a book than be warped by its attraction clean out of my own

orbit, and make a satellite out of a system. The one
thing in the world, of value, is the active soul.

What Emerson is talking about, in the terms I have used
in these pages, is the scribal rather than the knightly mode
of education, as his "bookworm" and his impatience with
received authority suggests. Emerson had himself received
and profited by that mode of education, as his writings amply testify. And he is himself a most telling example of the
shift from the scribal to the knightly type, which he typifies
better than any American of his day, and which, as we
shall see, ultimately triumphed in America. The figure of
the torch-relays from the first book of Plato's *Republic*
which has always been applied to the transmission of learning is, "Those that hold the torches pass them on, one man
to the next." The significant thing that is passed on is not
the piece of pitchy pine but the flame that it gives, which
may take on a new kind of intensity and give off a new
kind of light in the hand of each new runner.

Emerson's strictures may have contributed to the process
of maturation in American scholarship, one aspect of which
was emulation of developments in the universities of Europe. Emerson himself was a prime agent in convincing
Europe that American culture had come of age and was a
thing to be reckoned with, and the cultural traffic between
the old world and the new grew livelier. On the academic
side there was steady advance in the direction of advanced
study. American scholars were irked by dependence on
German universities, in which their own experiences had
not always been happy, and one graduate department after

another was established in American universities. Mainly because their founders were German-trained and the prestige of German universities was high, American graduate schools tended to follow the German pattern. The event that marked the relaxation of the leading strings was the Congress of Arts and Sciences held in connection with the Universal Exposition at St. Louis in 1904. The many volumes of the Proceedings of the Congress did not, as it was expected they would, revolutionize scholarship in many departments, but were rather in the nature of inventory and appraisal. But the Congress did assert America's coming of age in higher scholarship. Hugo Münsterberg described it as "the first great undertaking in which the Old and New Worlds stood on equal levels and in which Europe really became acquainted with the scientific life of these United States." A more ebullient observer wrote: "If civilized nations are the brain of humanity . . . the United States has become an independent lobe of the cortex in the course of the last forty years."

A concomitant of the new status of scholarship was a new regard for its teachers. Professors were not merely schoolmasters of higher degree, but members of a respected profession, and their genteel dress and manners distinguished them as such. And among all university teachers, those concerned with the classics enjoyed a special prestige. A man of large means who possessed scholarly tastes might choose the teaching of classics as a career. As late as 1920 the core of the classics department in at least one eastern university was a group of very wealthy men, and a teacher of Greek in a Brooklyn public high school regularly came to work in a chauffeur-driven Pierce-Arrow car.

It happens that the opulent men I have in mind were distinguished scholars and committed teachers, but their careers are evidence of the genteel status and untroubled existence associated with professors of Greek and Latin. Naturally, not all that were attracted to the calling were acute scholars or committed teachers.

Today, as a result of the partial eclipse of the classics, a greater percentage are. This is notably true of those who prepared for their calling during the depression years. It took courage to undertake a career in teaching at all, and it took foolhardiness to undertake one in a field where opportunities of employment were so few, and foolhardy men have spirit. Things are easier now; there are jobs, and they are decently paid. But despite black looks from my fellow teachers, I must confess that I am haunted by the vision of a young man weighing the attractions of teaching Greek against those of becoming a fireman, and choosing the Greek because the holidays are longer. We do not, of course, wish our people to starve, but willingness to starve did prove something. Despite our relative prosperity, we are still a university group with a cause. It is a great satisfaction to have a cause worth shivering a lance for, but the Don Quixotes of this world are expected to be indifferent to the contents of their saddlebags.

Between gentility and the scientific thoroughness adapted from the Germans, teaching of the classics in America after the Civil War fell to a low estate. The evidence comes from the memoirs of thoughtful observers who were by no means unfriendly to the classics, who did not gloat at the imminent fall of a senile tyrant, but who deplored the emasculation of what had been and could be a vital educational force.

I choose as a specimen some remarks of Nicholas Murray Butler, whom I knew as President of my own university, who had a complete understanding of what scholarship and teaching and education mean, and who could himself write very acceptable Latin. Recalling his undergraduate study of Greek, about 1870, under Professor Drisler (who held the chair I now occupy), President Butler wrote:

> [Drisler] was so given to insistence upon the minutest details of grammar that our eyes were kept closely fixed on the ground and we hardly ever caught any glimpse of the beauty and larger significance of the great works upon which we were engaged. For example, I recall that during the first term of the sophomore year we were to read with Dr. Drisler the *Medea* of Euripides and that when the term came to an end we had completed but 246 lines. In other words, we never came to know what the *Medea* was all about or to see either the significance of the story or the quality of its literary art.

Edward Delavan Perry, who was Drisler's successor and my own teacher, was a more imaginative and more amiable man; but by then the damage had been done, and in most of my classes with him I was the sole pupil. Somewhere between gentility and philology the undergraduate disappeared from view. Good secondary schools taught four years of Latin and three of Greek because good liberal arts colleges required that amount for admission. Students continued Latin and Greek in college because classics were required for an A.B. degree. I look with mingled emotions of awe and nostalgia and relief at the hundreds of "bare" texts of Xenophon and Lysias and Homer, to say nothing of Latin authors, stacked in our departmental cupboards, which were used for examinations. What an outcry there was, and what scorn, when some liberal arts colleges introduced a B.S. degree for which no Greek or Latin would be required, and what anguish when some colleges eliminated the requirement of Greek and Latin even for the A.B. degree!

It had to come. There were simply too many things that an educated man needed to know, whether the bachelor's was his terminal degree or whether he would proceed to professional or graduate study, for so large a segment of his time to be taken up. Furthermore (I say this with a feeling of guilt and with profound apology to men I revere) the actual classroom experience was so much more stimulating in other fields, that even if the student looked no farther than graduation, he might well feel that he could spend his undergraduate years more profitably in courses other than those in the classics. The definite break came with the stringency incident to World War I. In 1917, in my own and other colleges, Latin was removed from the list of required subjects. The examination texts were put into the cupboards, the younger teachers got jobs in banks, older men who could be absorbed into administrative work were employed in nonteaching capacities, and the departments of classics were staffed by those who remained. Their stream of students was reduced to a trickle, but never dried up. There were some who brought a propensity to classical study from home, there were some whose interest had been aroused by reading, specifically of translations of classics, and there were many who wished to carry on studies begun in secondary schools, in which study of the classics was not so quickly abandoned.

But soon the secondary schools, too, began the retreat; it could not be otherwise when the admissions offices of colleges no longer insisted on preparation in Latin. In the larger view the disappearance of Latin from the high school curriculum is more deplorable than its disappearance from college, and not merely because the college cannot do its best work unless students come with some preparation. In college, to put the matter briefly, there may be some doubt as to the claim of Latin vis-à-vis competing subjects; in the high school, I believe, there can be none. Latin is an ideal subject for the education of people of high school age.

Most high schools have, I am pleased to note, retained Latin, but in many, quantity and quality have been reduced. For one thing, there are not enough adequately prepared teachers. Some teachers' colleges teach their students how to teach Latin, but none that I know teaches them Latin. The traditional source of supply are college graduates who have a "major" in Latin, and who may have, in addition, taken courses in education or perhaps an M.A. in their subject. But with the elimination of Latin requirements, very few have taken "majors" in Latin in recent years. Furthermore, the program in many high schools has been reduced from four or three years to two, and the content in these two years much thinned. With only elementary work to teach, with qualified Latin teachers hard to find, and, in smaller schools, with not enough to occupy the teacher's full program, it frequently happens that a principal will assign the Latin work to a teacher of some other subject who has himself not gone beyond the elements in Latin. Some years ago, a devoted lady who was a professor in Hunter College made a habit of visiting high schools and encouraging the formation of Latin clubs, and the publication by these clubs of little Latin newspapers. After a few years, she felt impelled to retrace her travels in order to discourage the newspapers and clubs. The Latin in the newspapers had so deteriorated that they were considerably worse than none. The crowning touch was a visit to a school where the teacher proudly displayed a beautifully lettered sign which read *Fustis Latinus,* and when the visitor was obviously puzzled, the teacher explained, "Latin Club, of course." Of course, but only the kind of club you crack heads with.

The wave of uncomprehending pain which swept over the community of teachers of Greek and Latin when the earth beneath their feet was tottering, was pathetic. Some, who understood that the step was inevitable, thought it meant the end of education; many encased themselves in a cloak of private virtue, scorned the upstarts responsible for a return to barbarism, and waited for their injuries to be redressed. They could express their indignation only to one another, and in their isolation became more and more figures of fun to academic colleagues in other disciplines. It was only after the generation of the deluge had gone its way that professors of classics could be accepted as normal members of the academic community and participate in common deliberations without their colleagues raising their eyebrows or suppressing their smiles. We felt, in my early years, like frightened men who were merely being tolerated, ready to scamper at a sharp look. We were grateful to be allowed to keep classes much smaller than in other departments, so grateful indeed, that where a normal load of work was three classes, we took four. I must say at once, in justice to the administration, that no one did speak sharply to us or intentionally make us feel useless; we were our own scourge.

Our examination texts are still in the cupboard, but the situation has changed, in several directions, and all wholesome. Our classrooms, in my own and other institutions, are not overcrowded, but we do get more students, and what is more important, good ones. They are under no external pressure to study Greek and Latin; they study these difficult languages because they choose to, and so they do it well. Enough of them will proceed far enough in their study to carry on the tradition of scholarship, and all of them will retain knowledge and interest enough to keep the classical tradition alive as an integral part of our culture. An interesting index of the change of motivation is the altered numerical relationship between students of Greek and students of Latin. When pressure was applied, there was a great preponderance of Latin because Latin was thought to promote a professional career, or because Latin was thought easier. But when the sole motivation became a disinterested humanistic concern for literature and thought, there was a decided shift to Greek, because Greek has far the richer literature. So great has the preponderance of Greek become that whereas it is relatively easy to staff a college with teachers of Greek, it is more difficult to find college teachers whose major interest has been in Latin. Most satisfactory of all, perhaps, is the improved position of Latin in the high schools; Latin is recovering its proper place in one high school after another, and the work is of higher quality than it was a few years ago. Even Greek is showing signs of revival: the number of students offering Greek for admission to college is, for the first time since the twenties, gradually increasing.

The reasons for our newest revival are many; perhaps the simplest is that intelligent people will not wantonly abandon a precious part of the human legacy; and all literate people, even if they have not been taught the classical languages, are aware that the classics are indeed a valuable heritage. Our people are intelligent; to realize our shortcomings is of course a salutary thing, but surely we have estimated the cultural maturity of our people at too low a rate. The enormous public demand for good music is one piece of evidence; another and more convincing one is the enormous and unexpected circulation of "quality" paperback books. No one had believed that difficult books issued by university presses could have a larger audience than the minuscule editions that were printed, but some of the most abstruse works have proved the most successful.

A major factor in the revival of interest in the classical languages is the influence of classical works read in translation, in the Humanities course I have mentioned above and elsewhere. A word should be said about the propriety of using translations of classics and about the institution of Humanities courses. I have taught classics in translation and myself made a number of translations, and I have myself had a hand in shaping the pioneer Humanities course in Columbia College and have taught in it for many years, and so I shall speak of both from the viewpoint of my own experience.

For men of my generation, acceptance of translation as a legitimate avenue to understanding the classics involved something like apostasy. To teachers of the ancient languages there was something illicit and even obscene about a translation—it was a "pony" or a "trot" which only abandoned characters would resort to. In particular, interlinear translations, with the English equivalent printed above the Greek or Latin word, were regarded as an abomination and could be obtained only surreptitiously. For beginning students, the temptation to misuse translations was of course great and had to be guarded against. "Somebody else doing your translation," my teacher used to say, "does you no more good than somebody else eating your breakfast." For maturer students who want to learn, translations are a good device; they will of course not memorize the version but make sure they understand how the English, with its particular emphasis and tone, came out of the original. Macaulay used to take a Bible, in whatever new language he wished to learn, on an ocean voyage, and achieved his end if the voyage was long enough. He was in effect using a translation, for he carried the English text in his head.

My own conversion came as a result of my second year of college teaching. I had a class of five students in Euripides, of course in Greek, and prevailed upon my elders to let me do a class in Greek tragedy as a whole in translation, in which I had some twenty students. At examination time I thought it useless to examine the Euripides students in Greek—I had heard each of them recite at each class session—and gave them the questions on Euripides I had set for the course in English; after all, I had talked about things other than grammar and meter. What I found, when I read the blue books, was that the Euripides students had indeed learned some Greek, but gave no evidence that they had been stirred by a great artist's and thinker's probing into momentous questions of permanent relevance. The English students had, and I came to realize that teaching translations was not merely a device for filling my or the students' program with something intellectually frivolous, but was as important for fulfilling my function as teaching Greek.

My function is, as I conceive it, that of a curator of a trust. I must, of course, preserve the principal and if possible enlarge it, but I must also see that it reaches its intended beneficiaries; that, after all, is the ultimate object of the trust. I preserve the trust by raising up disciples to carry on my own work; I distribute its benefits by teaching. If I am not wholly successful in discharging these functions, I cannot be wholly a failure, for the books are the important thing, and work their effect regardless of their expounder. Actually, it has taken me many years to shed the feeling of guilt in working with translations, which many others could do as well, to the possible neglect of the things I had been trained to do. I did not finally shake the feeling off until all of my own teachers were retired, but I have continued with teaching translations and have gloried in it.

Translations of classics have become a considerable and respected part in the teaching of literature, largely through the Humanities courses I have yet to speak of, and groups of teachers who have had less experience in such work than I have sometimes asked me for what advice I could give.

Two or three years ago, I spoke to a meeting of college teachers of English in New England, suggesting authors, works, kinds of translation, approaches, and techniques which I had found useful. My audience was generally appreciative, but there were some who demurred at the whole enterprise. To the question whether books can actually be taught in translation, my one, and, I think, sufficient answer, is the Bible. Millions have read the Bible in modern languages untroubled by the thought that the original is in Hebrew and Greek, have understood it more fully than they could have done if they had known such rudiments of the languages as they might have acquired in school, have even written scholarly and perceptive things about it. One very eminent auditor protested that it was well enough to read Aeschylus in translation, but only in the junior or senior year, after the student has learned to read him in the original in his freshman and sophomore years. I answered that neither I nor my colleagues found it possible to teach even the most gifted students to read so difficult a poet as Aeschylus, with full and easy comprehension in the original Greek, in two years. Then, said he, neither should Aeschylus be read in translation, for to make a difficult thing seem easy is falsification. To this only one answer seemed possible, and that was that I and my colleagues loved people more than he and his colleagues did.

It was love of people, in the last analysis, that led to the institution of Humanities, which, from the limited arc of my own vision, was a significant turning point in American education. The originator, indirectly, was John Erskine, a Columbia professor of English who eventually became

head of the Juilliard School of Music. Erskine was a master
teacher who loved to talk, but loved as well to provoke
good talk. He noticed, about 1920, that the only zestful talk
about books to be heard on the campus was among students
in dormitory rooms, and thought the habit might be trans-
planted to classrooms also. Students who did advanced
directed reading in certain courses were enrolled in what
was called Special Honors. Erskine instituted a course called
General Honors. Each Wednesday evening at 7:30, a group
of twelve or fifteen students and two teachers would gather
round a table to discuss a book. The students were a select
group, the teachers were drawn from different departments,
the books were a selection of notable works from Homer
to modern times. The talk was good. In the matured judg-
ment of many who participated in it, the course was the
most valuable experience the college had to offer. Soon
the course was widely copied in adult education groups, first
under the leadership of Everett Dean Martin and with
Columbia staff in New York City and its suburbs, and eventually under the sponsorship of various groups the country
over. When, after some years, General Honors was abandoned at Columbia, faculty members who remembered it
from their undergraduate years insisted upon its restoration,
and it has continued, on a smaller scale but with undimin-
ished effectiveness, to this day. Its title, after its revival, is
Colloquium, and membership in the Colloquium, current
or past, carries a special cachet.

It was because the Colloquium was so desirable a thing
that the feeling arose, among those who loved their fellow
men, that its benefits should be more widely shared. After
long planning and debate, a two-year sequence to be called

Humanities and to be required of all undergraduates, was introduced. Resistance to the innovation was almost insuperable. How could a teacher, who could do only 300 lines of a play in a semester, do three plays in a week? How could authors, remote in time and place or abstruse in thought, be presented without long introduction? The objections were all sincere and some reasonable: Aristotle *is* abstruse, Milton *is* so richly allusive as to be caviare to the general. But all the books were written not for professors or graduate students but for people, and if all people could not plumb the full riches of every book, they could be enriched by what they could apprehend. In every section there are a few boys who are set afire by their discoveries, and a few virtually inaccessible to new ideas. But the middle reaches are all enriched and all have their minds stretched, each according to his native elasticity. The one legitimate fear was that we might be producing self-assured sciolists, boys who after a week's exposure to St. Augustine or Dante would assume that they knew everything worth knowing about these authors. That has happily proven not to be the case. No teacher claims omniscience, and his humility is communicated to his students. The best antidote to smugness, however, is the fact that the students also have rigorous courses where no charm or facility with words will do; if I did not know that my students were studying mathematics at the same time, I myself should be dubious about the merits of Humanities.

The question of drawing up the initial list also presented difficulties. Individual departments wavered between eagerness to have their own masterpieces introduced and dread of having these masterpieces treated too summarily. I recall the quandary of the group in discussing the candidacy of Goethe's *Faust*. Our professor of German was naturally an enthusiastic admirer of *Faust* but also a man with high blood pressure: would he be more likely to be struck with apoplexy if *Faust* were omitted, or if *Faust* were trampled over in one week? A more important factor was diffidence at drawing up any list which would take on the aspect of a canon. We do make it clear to our students that the list is by no means exclusive: these happen to be the books convenient for our purposes, but there are others equally worthy. In point of fact, the list is actually changed somewhat from year to year, and the students know that it is. On the other hand, the list that was published under the title *Classics of the Western World,* is so inclusive that only a fraction of it can be handled in any given year; it is too large to be taken as a canon.

It is with a list of some thirty books that the first year of our Humanities course is taken up. Of the second year one term is devoted to music and the other to fine arts. None of the courses are "surveys" of the traditional sort, and no anthologies or secondary works are used. Each course proceeds by direct study of a particular monument, to which three or four class meetings are devoted. Classes are kept to a maximum of twenty or so. The first part of the course is taught by the same instructor, whatever his department, throughout the year; the music and fine arts are taught by specialists in those fields. In some institutions which have a similar program, the same teacher handles not only the literature and philosophy but the music and fine arts also. Some institutions make the work of each section in the first year different, according to the tastes of the instructor. Our

Columbia course has a uniform reading list and uniform examinations, but what one man does in his class may be very different from what another does, and, hopefully, very different from what he himself has done or may do another year. Not the least of the effects of the course is the education of the instructors. Each has special competence in a particular field, training for which may have blinded him to other areas. The Humanities course makes humanists not only of the untaught, but also of those who may have been taught too much.

Some institutions organize their humanities work in a separate department, with a staff and a budget of its own. This I think undesirable, for I cannot think that one man can encompass all the knowledge that would entitle him to be called a professor of humanities. It is better, I believe, to have staff drawn from the various appropriate departments, and for members to meet weekly with a chairman chosen from among the senior members of the group and serving for a limited term. These meetings not only handle routine administrative business but listen to individual appreciations of given elements of the book currently dealt with, suggested procedures for teaching the book, or perhaps an informal talk by some member who has special competence in the subject.

Though the professors of classics were the ones to resist the introduction of humanities longest and most intensely, the literatures they represent occupy, through no efforts of theirs, the lion's share of the whole reading list. And however much the list changes, the classical books remain. To a humanist, of course, nothing could be more rational or more gratifying. Thucydides was much admired in antiquity and in the modern world since the Renaissance, but it may be that more people have read Thucydides in the various Great Books courses in this country than had ever read him before. And this is as it should be, for there is no better or more economical or more agreeable way to learn about the political behavior of men and states. I would hazard the guess that Americans educated in the last two decades know no playwright aside from Shakespeare as well as they know Sophocles, and that too is as it should be, for no other playwright, not excluding Shakespeare himself, offers such mature and timeless wisdom in so concentrated a form.

I look on and am content, as I think Isocrates or the Renaissance humanists would be content. We do discharge our obligations to the scribal mode of education, as it is important we should. Our graduate professors carry on research at a high level and train successors to carry their work forward. Their work is respected by colleagues in other fields and by the literate public, and it receives material support. Within recent months, newspapers carried accounts of a generous endowment for an institute of advanced study in Greek in Washington, and of another in Cincinnati. During the lean thirties, when undergraduates would consult me about the prospects and possibilities for graduate work in Greek, I would felicitate them upon their choice but felt obliged, as a responsible citizen, to warn them that support for advanced work would be hard to find, and employment, after they received the doctorate, by no means certain. Happily neither difficulty obtains. Young men and women who love the classics can proceed to graduate training with no more sacrifice than is demanded of students in other nonscientific fields, and have as reasonable

a chance for satisfactory employment. The part of the curator's task which has to do with preservation and transmission is being attended to.

But if the scribal ideal survives and flourishes, it is no
longer, thanks to such innovations as the Humanities
courses, sole and exclusive. The knightly ideal is supported
even by the scribes; they not only preserve and transmit to
future scribes, but they also strive to transmit the legacy
to as many of its intended beneficiaries as they can reach.
If among the recipients of the legacy, the proportion of those
who know the ancient books in their original tongues is
small, there is compensation in the thought that the proportion of our whole people who are able to participate in
the legacy is larger than it has ever before been. The knightly
ideal is no longer restricted to knights but has been made
accessible to every man—or better, every man is now a
knight. That is the essential value of democracy; neither in
Rome nor, probably, in England was humanistic learning
so widely distributed as it was in the Athenian democracy,
and I do not think that it was as widely distributed in the
Athenian democracy as it is in our own. The men of the
Renaissance took up where the ancients left off and made
humanism viable and vigorous. In my own time, I feel,
though less spectacularly, we have taken up and given new
vigor to the impulse which the Renaissance initiated. It is
good for us and good for the world, and I am pleased to
have been a part of it.

At the end of his career, Thomas Hardy wrote a poem
he called "An Ancient to Ancients." Because his conclud-

ing words express my mood better than any of mine could
do, I should like to transcribe them here:

> *Sophocles, Plato, Socrates,*
> > *Gentlemen,*
> *Pythagoras, Thucydides,*
> *Herodotus, and Homer,—yea,*
> *Clement, Augustin, Origen*
> *Burnt brightlier towards their setting-day,*
> > *Gentlemen.*
>
> *And ye, red-lipped and smooth-browed; list,*
> > *Gentlemen;*
> *Much is there waits you we have missed;*
> *Much lore we leave you worth the knowing,*
> *Much, much has lain outside our ken:*
> *Nay, rush not; time serves; we are going,*
> > *Gentlemen.*